Jesus Farewell Address

John 14–16
Bible Commentary

Andrew Wommack

All emphasis within Scripture quotations is the author's own.

Published in partnership between Andrew Wommack Ministries and Harrison House Publishers.

Woodland Park, CO 80863 – Shippensburg, PA 17257

ISBN 13 TP: 978-1-59548-700-1

For Worldwide Distribution, Printed in the USA

1 2 3 4 5 6 / 27 26 25 24

CONTENTS

INTRODUCTION

The fourteenth, fifteenth, and sixteenth chapters of the Gospel of John record the last time Jesus ministered to His disciples before His crucifixion. The disciples were about to enter a crisis where they would see Jesus arrested, beaten, crucified, dead, and buried, and these were His final instructions to them.

I know that sometimes a person's perspective can view a minor issue as a major crisis. And yet, some of you are truly in a critical situation. What you're going through could be life-threatening. It could be problems in your marriage, business, or finances. But I don't believe anybody is facing a crisis like these disciples faced.

From their perspective, it looked like all the hopes they had put in Jesus as the Messiah—that He was going to redeem Israel and deliver them from the Roman occupation—were just totally wrong. Not only were their hopes dashed spiritually and emotionally, but they were also in danger physically.

All four gospels highlight the fact that Peter denied the Lord three times (Matt. 26:69–75, Mark 14:66–72, Luke 22:54–62, and John 18:16–18, 25–27), but *all* the disciples forsook Him and fled (Matt. 26:56). They believed their lives were in jeopardy. But look at what Jesus told His disciples the night He was arrested. The very first thing He said to them, as recorded in John 14:1, was, "*Let not your heart be troubled.*" I'll tell you, that is just phenomenal!

Often, in the United States, our presidents give a final speech to the nation before leaving office. Men like George Washington, Dwight Eisenhower, and Ronald Reagan took time to recount the successes of their term, remind the people of what makes America great, warn them of challenges ahead, and generally encourage the nation. This kind of speech is called a "farewell address." In a sense, John 14–16 was Jesus' farewell address.

After spending three years following Jesus, His disciples were entrusted with carrying on His ministry. And yet, they didn't know where He was going or who He really was (John 14:5-9). It's no wonder they were called "duh-sciples"!

Jesus' disciples needed a reminder from Him of what they'd seen, who He was, what was to come, and how it would turn out. Most of all, they needed encouragement!

As you read through these chapters, you are going to see some of the most amazing things Jesus taught. And I believe the things He shared are just as important for us today as they were two thousand years ago.

This book contains just a portion of the twenty-seven thousand footnotes I've written in my *Living Commentary* on the entire Bible. We call it the *Living Commentary* because I am still writing it. It is a digital study bible and commentary and every time someone who has purchased it logs in to the software or on the website, it automatically provides the newest notes I've published.

This book and the *Living Commentary* also include notes originally written for our *Life for Today Study Bible and Commentary: Gospels Edition*, which we published years ago and is no longer being updated. The individual notes are presented with *Living Commentary* notes first, followed by *Life for Today* notes, and separated by lines.

If you haven't purchased my *Living Commentary*, I strongly recommend it. In my opinion, it is the best product I've ever offered. I've been studying the Word of God for more than fifty-six years and this commentary reflects all the revelations the Lord has given me. I've spent hours and even days writing some of these notes and I believe these truths will change your life, as they have mine.

While you read through this book, you may notice that some of the notes may seem to repeat themselves. I want you to know that while these things may be taken from the same revelation, they are often written from a different perspective. I encourage you to take the time to read each one of these notes and meditate on the truths the Lord has revealed to me. You'll be blessed!

John Chapter 14

John 14:1

Let not your heart be troubled: ye believe in God, believe also in me.

Remember the context. In the previous verse (John 13:38), Jesus had just told Peter that he would deny Him three times before the rooster crowed in the morning. But despite that, Jesus was telling Peter and the rest of the disciples not to let their hearts be troubled.

The understood subject of this verse is "you." It's up to us to control our hearts. It's God's power that makes that possible, but we have to make the choice and draw on God's ability. How do we do that? This verse goes on to say, "*Believe in God.*" Faith is how we conquer our emotions.

Jesus made these statements to His disciples the night before His crucifixion. Even in those extreme circumstances, Jesus was telling them not to let their hearts be troubled. That's amazing. And that reveals the authority we have over our emotions. The Lord would have been unjust to command His disciples to do something that they were powerless to do. Therefore, we can control our emotions regardless of how things are going.

The fact that Jesus mentioned controlling our emotions first in this list of all the things we should do is also significant. If we let our emotions run away with us, then it's nearly impossible to rein them in. It's easier to hold them at bay than it is to stop them once we have let them go. Harnessing our emotions is the first thing to do in a crisis situation. Most battles are won or lost in the first few moments, according to the way we allow our emotions to go.

The understood subject of this sentence is "you." "You" let not your heart be troubled. You are the one who has control of your heart. Other people and circumstances cannot trouble you unless you allow them to divert your attention from the Lord and His Word (Is. 26:3; see notes at John 14:27).

Jesus had just told the disciples not to let their hearts be troubled, and here He told them how to do it. Believe! Faith in God is the victory that overcomes the world and all its troubles (1 John 5:4).

The disciples believed in Jesus enough to be totally devastated when He died but not enough to believe His prophecies concerning His resurrection (Matt. 16:21). Jesus made it very clear in this same teaching (John 16:1) that He was saying these things so that His disciples would not be offended, but His words didn't profit them, because they didn't mix them with faith (Heb. 4:2). They had enough faith to be dissatisfied with failure but not enough to have victory. It's better to go all the way in believing God than just part way.

John 14:2

> *In my Father's house are many mansions: if* it were *not* so, *I would have told you. I go to prepare a place for you.*

Jesus had just told His disciples not to let their hearts be troubled as they were about to enter into the worst crisis of their lives (John 14:1). Here, He began to speak about heaven. What does heaven have to do with believers keeping their hearts at peace?

Well, even if everything in this life looks terrible, we Christians always have the promise of total victory in heaven. If every time we think we see light at the end of the tunnel and it turns out to be another train, then we can always just close our eyes and think about our great reward in heaven. That will keep our hearts from being troubled.

This was Jesus' last teaching to His disciples before His crucifixion. Jesus' disciples were about to go through the greatest test of their faith that they had ever encountered. According to John 16:1 (which is a part of this same teaching), Jesus said that He was saying these things so that His disciples would not be offended. Jesus was preparing them for what was to come. Why then speak of preparing them a mansion in heaven?

The reason for this was to comfort the disciples and help them put things in perspective. In 1 Thessalonians 4:17–18,

Paul told us to comfort one another with words about being gathered unto the Lord in the air. Paul also said, "*I reckon that the sufferings of this present time* are *not worthy* to be compared *with the glory which shall be revealed in us*" (Rom. 8:18).

Someday, all of our trials will seem like nothing, and that can be a great comfort to us now.

Also, thinking about being with the Lord through all eternity helps put things in a proper perspective. It is easy to get fearful in our problems and think all is lost. However, for those of us who are born again, if worse came to worse, we still have the promise of Jesus wiping all the tears from our eyes (Rev. 21:4) and preparing a habitation for us where all the former sorrows will be passed away. This keeps us from despairing and makes us much stronger in our faith.

The Greek word used for "*house*" is *oikia*, and it means "residence ... an abode."[1] This verse is simply stating that in heaven, there are many dwelling places, and Jesus is preparing one for us. The use of the word "*mansions*" certainly denotes that we will be taken care of in fine fashion, but from this one passage, it cannot be said emphatically that we will all have private residences or exactly what they will be like. We can only see faintly now, like looking through a dark glass (1 Cor. 13:12), but we can be assured that it will be more than we could ever ask or think (Eph. 3:20).

John 14:3

> *And if I go and prepare a place for you, I will come again, and receive you unto myself; that where I am,* there *ye may be also.*

It only took the Lord seven days to create the heavens and the earth (Gen. 2:1–2). He has been working on our mansions for 2,000 years. These mansions must be something great.

Jesus was saying these things about heaven to keep the disciples' hearts from being troubled as they entered the darkest period of their lives. This also revealed how Jesus kept from being discouraged during the darkest period of His own life. It all centered around thinking about eternity. His attention was focused on the joy that was set before Him (Heb. 12:2–3). It can only be done when we put things into their proper perspective in light of eternity.

This world is not all there is. There is eternity, and the time we spend in eternity and the benefits we receive there will far outweigh all concerns that happen here on earth (Rom. 8:18). If we only have hope in this world, then we will be the most miserable of all people (1 Cor. 15:19). To have the positive faith that Jesus exhibited and that He is commanding us to have here, we have to be heavenly minded (Col. 3:1–2).

The thing that is going to make heaven "heaven" is the fact that we will be with Jesus. No doubt there will be things to see and do that will be wonderful, but nothing will compare with being with the one who loved us and died for us. A preoccupation with the details of what things will be like in heaven is missing this point.

John 14:4

And whither I go ye know, and the way ye know.

Jesus was not asking a question but rather making a statement. He said they did know where He was going and how to get there. However, Thomas contradicted Him, saying, "We don't know where You are going, and if we don't know that, how can we know the way to where You are going?" Who was right, Jesus or Thomas?

Jesus went on to explain in John 14:6 that He was going to His Father and that He was the only way to approach unto the Father. Jesus had already explained these things to His disciples before; they just failed to make the connection. So Jesus, of course, was the one who was correct. He always is. Likewise, we may not understand something the Lord has said in His Word, but we should never take the position of contradicting it like Thomas and later Philip (John 14:8) did. It is all right to seek clarification or explanation (see notes at John 14:22), but we should never trust in our own understanding more than in God's Word (Prov. 3:5).

John 14:5

Thomas saith unto him, Lord, we know not whither thou goest; and how can we know the way?

When the Lord says we know something, it would be smart to just keep our mouths shut and not make fools of ourselves

(Prov. 17:28). But Thomas opened his mouth and stuck his foot in it. In fact, with a number of Jesus' disciples, it seemed like the only time they opened their mouths was to change feet.

Thomas knew Jesus; he just didn't realize Jesus was the way. Likewise, people today know portions of God's Word, but they don't realize that God's Word is their way to victory. Often, people cry out for God to speak to them while their Bibles lie unopened on their nightstands. God has spoken to people through His Word (Matt. 11:7). They just need to believe it and receive its truths as their way to victory.

John 14:6

> *Jesus saith unto him, I am the way, the truth, and the life: no man cometh unto the Father, but by me.*

This means there are not many paths to God. Jesus is the only way, truth, and life. There is no other way. There is no other truth but the truths Jesus gave us. There is no other life except through Jesus, the Creator of life (John 1:4). Christianity is not just another religion. It is God's only method of salvation (Acts 4:12). Hinduism, Buddhism, Islam, and all other religions are therefore not of God but of man and the devil. Those who trust in those religions will be eternally damned.

Jesus didn't say "I am *a* way, *a* truth, and *a* life." He claimed to be *the only* way, truth, and life. No person can come to the Father except through Jesus. This means that anyone who claims to honor Jesus while advocating other ways to God, to truth, or to life besides Jesus is deceived or a deceiver. Jesus' claims about Himself, of which this is only one, left no room for other means of salvation (John 10:1, 8). He was either who He said He was, or He was the greatest deceiver of all time. His own statements about Himself leave no other alternatives. Therefore, other religions that recognize Jesus and His teachings as wonderful examples but don't believe He is the only way to achieve salvation are false.

Jesus said later this same night, "*Thy word is truth*" (John 17:17). Jesus and God's Word are one (John 1:1, 14; 1 John 5:7; Rev. 19:13). Anything that doesn't agree with God's Word doesn't agree with Jesus and vice versa. In Jesus are hid all the treasures of wisdom and knowledge (Col. 2:3).

John 14:7

> *If ye had known me, ye should have known my Father also: and from henceforth ye know him, and have seen him.*

Knowing Jesus is knowing the Father because They are one (John 10:30 and 1 Tim. 3:16). Jesus was the express image of the Father (Heb. 1:3). There is zero difference between the two. These disciples knew Jesus in a sense but not really. They didn't know what they had. But Jesus was telling them that in a short while, after He was resurrected from the dead, they would realize who He really was.

Knowing Jesus is knowing the Father. This is not only because Jesus did exactly what He saw His Father do (John 5:19 and 8:29) but also because Jesus was God in the flesh (1 Tim. 3:16 and John 18:19).

Once again, Jesus made a statement of fact, but this time Philip challenged Him (compare with my notes at John 14:4). The disciples did know Jesus, and they of course had seen Him. However, they didn't realize that seeing Jesus was seeing God. They were expecting something more. Many times, we miss seeing God at work in our lives and circumstances because we are looking for something stupendous.

Although it is true that God is totally awesome, He doesn't usually choose to manifest Himself that way. God spoke to Elijah not in the wind or earthquake or fire, but in a still, small voice (1 Kgs. 19:11–13).

Jesus didn't come to this earth in a grand way by man's standards but was born to poor parents in a stable. Isaiah 53:2 says that Jesus had no form nor beauty that would make us think that He was anything more than a mere man. Paul revealed in 1 Corinthians 1:27–29 that God chooses to do things this way so that no flesh should glory in His presence.

The Lord wants us to focus on Him through faith and not concentrate on the physical things He uses. In the Old Testament when the Lord did use visible instruments to release His power, the Israelites made idols out of those things

(Num. 21:6–9 with 2 Kgs. 18:4). Just as these disciples had seen Jesus but didn't realize who they had seen was God, likewise, God is infinitely involved in our everyday lives. But we miss Him because we are blinded by our carnal minds (1 Cor. 2:14; compare with my notes at John 14:5).

John 14:8

Philip saith unto him, Lord, shew us the Father, and it sufficeth us.

Get this! Philip was looking at God manifested in the flesh (1 Tim. 3:16), and he wasn't satisfied. If Jesus doesn't satisfy, what or who does? Philip thought seeing the heavens open and being able to look at God seated on the throne would be enough, but Jesus said seeing Him was as good as seeing the Father. What a statement!

We can't know God in just physical terms. We have to know God by and through the Spirit. God is a Spirit, and those who worship Him must worship Him in spirit and in truth (John 4:24). If they had known Jesus in spirit, they would have longed for nothing more. He was every bit God; they just didn't realize what they had.

Philip was basically asking for the same thing that Moses asked for in Exodus 33:18–34:8. The difference was that Moses didn't have Jesus standing in front of him and Philip did. Jesus is the express image of the Father (Heb. 1:3). There is no greater manifestation of God than what Jesus gave us. Having the heavens open and seeing God the Father isn't better than looking at God through Jesus.

And it's not the physical flesh of Jesus that revealed the express image of God. Jesus was just the body that Christ inhabited. It was the actions and words of Jesus that revealed the true Christ. We can get that same revelation by seeing Jesus through the Word with the revelation knowledge of the Holy Spirit. We don't have to ask, nor do we need to see anything more than Jesus (John 20:29).

We tend to think that if the Lord would just do this or that, then we would be satisfied, but that is not so. The flesh can never be satisfied. It has an insatiable lust like a person with a drug addiction. What provided assurance at one time ceases to do so, and there has to be another "fix." Faith in the revelation that God has already given (i.e., the Word of God) is the only way to a "crutch-free" relationship with the Father (Luke 16:31).

John 14:9

> *Jesus saith unto him, Have I been so long time with you, and yet hast thou not known me, Philip? he that hath seen me hath seen the Father; and how sayest thou* then, *Shew us the Father?*

Just like Philip, most of us don't fully know what we have in Jesus. Those twelve disciples were at a disadvantage. They had Jesus in His physical form. Jesus was totally God in His heart, but His physical body was natural, with no beauty that made Him desirable (Is. 53:2).

It was difficult for them to look past Jesus' physical body and see His true self within. We don't have that problem. We can close our eyes and see Jesus seated at the Father's right hand in glory and power. It is easier for us to perceive who Jesus really is than it was for the disciples. What a reversal of the way most people think.

1 Samuel 16:7 says, "*But the Lord said unto Samuel, Look not on his countenance, or on the height of his stature; because I have refused him: for* the Lord seeth *not as man seeth; for man looketh on the outward appearance, but the Lord looketh on the heart.*"

People tend to look on the exterior instead of the true heart of a person. That is the root of all prejudice and bigotry. Paul said, "*Wherefore henceforth know we no man after the flesh: yea, though we have known Christ after the flesh, yet now henceforth know we* him *no more*" (2 Cor. 5:16).

It is possible to know a lot about a person and yet not know that person. The disciples had spent years with Jesus and had seen more of His works than anyone, yet they didn't really know Him. Knowing about Jesus will not suffice for knowing Jesus when we stand before God's throne (James 2:19; John 7:28, 8:32, and 10:27).

John 14:10

> *Believest thou not that I am in the Father, and the Father in me? the words that I speak unto you I speak not of myself: but the Father that dwelleth in me, he doeth the works.*

This is a great mystery: how Jesus could be in the Father and yet the Father be in Him. Our finite minds can't comprehend this. Anything big enough to contain us is too big to be inside us. Apparently, space isn't the same in the spiritual realm.

Or possibly Jesus was speaking about His Father being in Him in the sense that we say, "I have you in my heart" (Phil. 1:7) when we are referring to having feelings for someone.

Jesus only spoke what He heard His Father speak, and then the Father did the works or miracles. That's the way it works for us. We must hear what the Lord wants us to say. Then when we speak God's words without doubting (Mark 11:23), the Father does the work.

John 14:11

> *Believe me that I* am *in the Father, and the Father in me: or else believe me for the very works' sake.*

Jesus made this same point in John 5:36: "*But I have greater witness than* that *of John: for the works which the Father hath given me to finish, the same works that I do, bear witness of me, that the Father hath sent me.*"

He also made this same point in John 10:37–38, saying, *"If I do not the works of my Father, believe me not. But if I do, though ye believe not me, believe the works: that ye may know, and believe, that the Father* is *in me, and I in him."*

Jesus' logic is recorded three times in the Gospel of John. John 10:37–38, as well as Jesus' statement here, show there are two ways to believe. We can believe God's Word, or we can believe because we see what God's Word produces. The greater blessing is on believing God's Word (John 20:29).

Jesus here stated two bases for people's faith in Him. They can either believe in Him because of all the evidence or believe in Him just because of His Word. Jesus put the greater blessing on those who make His Word the basis of their faith (John 20:29; Matt. 8:10 and 11:7). He went on to declare in John 14:12 that those who base their faith on Him alone will be able to produce the same works that He did and even greater.

John 14:12

Verily, verily, I say unto you, He that believeth on me, the works that I do shall he do also; and greater works *than these shall he do; because I go unto my Father.*

What a wonderful promise! We can do the same works that Jesus did! Thank You, Jesus! Some people have focused on the greater works and forgotten Jesus said we would do the same works that He did. He healed the sick, cleansed the lepers, and raised the dead. He made blind eyes see and deaf ears hear. He made the lame walk. We can and should be doing these same works. God hasn't changed (Heb. 13:8). It's the people representing Him who have changed. Until we accomplish these same works that Jesus did, we shouldn't worry about trying to do the greater works.

This scripture makes it very clear that it is God's plan to do the same miraculous deeds through believers as He did through Jesus. The only reason we don't see more miracles today is not because God doesn't will to do them but rather because very few believe. Through those who believe, God is still healing the sick, raising the physically dead to physical life again, casting out devils, and taking charge of the elements, as He did through Jesus and the apostles in the Bible days. This scripture will never fit into a theology that says miracles are not for today.

Some people have tried to avoid the obvious teaching about miracles in this verse by focusing attention on Jesus' statement that believers would do greater works than Him. They say that preaching the Gospel over radio and television and the printed page are these greater works because they are reaching more people than Jesus ever did. Even if these were the greater works that Jesus referred to, that would not void Jesus' statement in this same sentence that believers would do the same works that He did. This verse makes it very clear that as long as there are believers, the same miraculous power that the Word recorded operating through Jesus will also operate through those who believe. Failure to see the miraculous power of God in our lives is our fault, not God's.

There are special ministry gifts of the Spirit (1 Cor. 12:8–10), such as the gift of miracles, that only some people possess. But this verse is stating that every believer can do the same miracles that Jesus did and even greater. Therefore, some people may not have a ministry of miracles, but through their own faith, they can see them operate in their lives as they have need of them.

What are these "*greater*" works that Jesus spoke of? It is clear in Scripture that Jesus had the Spirit without measure, or in an unlimited amount (John 1:14 and 3:34), so how could anyone possibly do anything greater than what Jesus did? Some people have thought that Jesus might have been referring to the fact that believers are able to reach more people with the Gospel and the miraculous power of God than what He was able to do in His brief ministry here on earth (see notes at John 14:12). It is also possible that Jesus didn't perform every possible type of miracle, and if there arose the need, His disciples could. Also, the new birth, that Jesus spoke of (John 3:3–7) and came to provide by His death and resurrection, was not yet a reality (John 3:10). Therefore, it is possible that this miracle of the new birth was considered by Jesus to be greater than all the physical miracles that He had performed.

Why did Jesus hinge the ability of those who believed on Him to perform these miracles on the fact that He was going unto the Father? Jesus later revealed, in this same discourse, that the Holy Spirit could not come until Jesus had departed to the Father (John 16:7; see also 7:39). It was through the anointing power of the Holy Spirit that Jesus' miracles had occurred. As spoken in Zechariah 4:6, "not by might, nor by power, but by my spirit, saith the Lord of hosts." Therefore, without the baptism of the Holy Spirit and the power that it brings (Acts 1:8), these miracles cannot occur.

John 14:13

> *And whatsoever ye shall ask in my name, that will I do, that the Father may be glorified in the Son.*

Asking in the name of Jesus is more than just words. This is speaking of asking and expecting to receive solely on account of what Jesus did for us. It is not coming to the Father on the basis of any worth or merit of our own but putting total faith in what Jesus did for us. Those who simply say "in Jesus' name" but then proclaim their own worth or are condemned because of their unworthiness are not truly coming to the Father in the name of Jesus.

Jesus expounded on this truth later in this same discourse with His disciples that same night (John 16:23–25). Going directly to the Father with their prayers in the name of Jesus had never been done before (see my notes at John 16:23–24).

If the previous promise didn't convince the disciples that the Father would accomplish the same miracles through them as He had through Jesus, then this one should have. Jesus reiterated the truth of John 14:12 in different words, thereby underscoring the certainty of this promise. Then in John 14:14, He repeated this same promise again. It was very uncharacteristic of Jesus to repeat Himself three times in immediate succession. This must, no doubt, be interpreted as Jesus assuring His disciples that this seemingly unbelievable promise was, in fact, true. As explained in Hebrews 6:17–18, God did the same thing with Abraham. Anyone who would doubt the statement of John 14:12 because of it being such a departure from the norm could not, in a pure heart, doubt the meaning of Jesus' three statements when taken as a whole.

John 14:14

If ye shall ask any thing in my name, I will do it.

There are certain qualifications to this promise even though they aren't stated here. Matthew 21:22 says, "*And all things, whatsoever ye shall ask in prayer, believing, ye shall receive.*"

And James 1:6–7 says, "*But let him ask in faith, nothing wavering. For he that wavereth is like a wave of the sea driven with the wind and tossed. For let not that man think that he shall receive any thing of the Lord.*"

Therefore, faith is a prerequisite to receiving, whether stated or not. We also have to ask for things according to God's will (1 John 5:14–15), which is His Word. We can't just get whatever we want. We might want some things that are bad for us, and the Lord will not grant those things, just as good parents will not give their children whatever they want (James 4:2–3). The Lord has already provided every good thing we will ever need. It's a part of Christ's atonement. Faith only appropriates what God has already provided by grace. So, if it isn't already provided through Christ, we can't get it through prayer and faith (Eph. 2:8).

These awesome promises of miraculous power through faith must never be taken and applied in any way that is contrary to the rest of Scripture, or they will not work (Matt. 7:7).

John 14:15

If ye love me, keep my commandments.

Keeping the commandments doesn't produce loving God. But loving God will produce keeping His commandments. There's a big difference between those two approaches. The Lord gave us a new commandment to love each other as He loves us (John 13:34). And this commandment supersedes all the other commandments.

The way that most Christians have interpreted this verse is an example of spiritual dyslexia (a disorder that can cause a seeming reversal of words when reading). Jesus did not say that keeping His commandments would cause us to love Him but rather loving Him would cause us to keep His commandments. This same thing is true of John's statements in 1 John 2:3–4.

John 14:16

> *And I will pray the Father, and he shall give you another Comforter, that he may abide with you for ever;*

The Greek word *allos*, which was translated "*another*" in this verse, is in contrast with the Greek word heteros, which means "another of a different sort." "*Allos* expresses a numerical difference and denotes 'another of the same sort.' ... Christ promised to send 'another Comforter' (...'another like Himself'...)"[2] The Holy Spirit is another Comforter just like Jesus. Jesus said it was actually to our advantage to have the ministry of the Holy Spirit rather than His personal presence (John 16:7).

The Holy Spirit was separate from Jesus, as can be seen in the fact that the Holy Spirit descended on Jesus at His baptism in a bodily shape as a dove (Matt. 3:16, Mark 1:10, and Luke 3:22). Yet the Holy Spirit was referred to as God in Acts 5:3–4. In light of the declaration of Deuteronomy 6:4 that "*the LORD our God* is *one Lord*," this is a great mystery that the church has called the Trinity.

Remember that Jesus was saying these things to His disciples so that they would not be offended (see notes at John 14:2). In John 14:16–27, Jesus was speaking to His disciples about the Holy Spirit, who is the Comforter. The ministry of the Holy Spirit in the life of the believer is the front line of defense against the devil and his devices of defeat.

The Holy Spirit was active in the Old Testament, but the ministry of the Holy Spirit to the New Testament believer has some major differences. One of these differences is that once the believer receives the Holy Spirit, He remains forever. During the Old Testament days, the Holy Spirit came and went in (1 Pet. 1:11) and among people. David expressed fear about God taking His Holy Spirit from him (Ps. 51:11). This is in sharp contrast with promises of the New Testament (this verse Rom. 8:35–39, Eph. 1:13–14, and Heb. 13:5).

John 14:17

> Even *the Spirit of truth; whom the world cannot receive, because it seeth him not, neither knoweth him: but ye know him; for he dwelleth with you, and shall be in you.*

Anyone who hasn't been born again cannot be baptized in the Holy Spirit. That's what Jesus was saying when He said that the world cannot receive the Holy Spirit. Non-Christians can't receive anything beyond their five senses (1 Cor. 2:14). They are super limited. They can't walk by faith (2 Cor. 5:7).

The Holy Spirit was referred to as "*the Spirit of truth*" three times in this last discourse from Jesus to His disciples (this verse, and vv. 15:26 and 16:13).

Jesus' statement here that the world cannot receive the Holy Spirit is very important. This means that until people are born again (John 3:3), they cannot receive the Holy Spirit. Unbelievers cannot receive the baptism of the Holy Spirit. Peter used this as a proof of salvation in Acts 11:15–17.

People, apart from the quickening of the Holy Spirit, cannot believe what they cannot see. Paul said in 1 Corinthians 2:14, "*But the natural man receiveth not the things of the Spirit of God: for they are foolishness unto him: neither can he know* them, *because they are spiritually discerned.*"

This is why lost people cannot receive the Holy Spirit.

Jesus made a clear distinction between the Holy Spirit being with the disciples and being in them. The ministry of the Holy Spirit is always involved in all of God's dealings with man. This was certainly true of the Lord's revelation to the disciples of who Jesus was. However, the Holy Spirit had only so far been with them, but He would soon be in them. Likewise, today some may claim that they have the Holy Spirit because of the fact that no one can come to Jesus except through the ministry of the Holy Spirit (John 6:44). But only through the baptism of the Holy Spirit does He actually come and live in the hearts of the believers.

John 14:18

I will not leave you comfortless: I will come to you.

The Greek word *orphanos*, which was translated "*comfortless*" in this verse, means "bereaved ('orphan'), i.e. parentless."[3] Jesus actually said He would not leave us bereaved as orphans. Thank You, Jesus.

In John 14:16–17, Jesus had clearly spoken of the Holy Spirit coming and dwelling in the disciples. Here He spoke of Himself coming to the disciples in the same context. Referring to Himself and the Holy Spirit interchangeably in these verses stressed the oneness of Jesus and the Holy Spirit and the place of the Holy Spirit in the Godhead (Mark 1:10).

John 14:19

Yet a little while, and the world seeth me no more; but ye see me: because I live, ye shall live also.

The English word "*see*" in here was translated from the Greek word *theoreo*, which was translated by a number of English words. It was translated "*perceive*" four times (John 4:19 and 12:19; Acts 17:22 and 27:10).[4] It was also translated "*consider*" in Hebrews 7:4, which says, "*Now consider how great this man* was, *unto whom even the patriarch Abraham gave the tenth of the spoils.*"

This Greek word differs from the dominant Greek word, *eido*, which was translated "see" in the New Testament. It is referring to just "mechanical, passive, or casual vision."[5] The thought of this verse is that the time was coming when the unbelievers wouldn't be able to perceive Jesus because they only looked with physical eyes. But Christ's true followers could perceive Jesus because they could perceive Him in their hearts. How would Jesus' true followers be able to perceive Him? In John 14:21, Jesus said those who loved Him enough to obey Him would be loved by Himself and His Father, and Jesus would manifest Himself to them.

This is a reference to His crucifixion, only a few hours away. From that time on, the world (the unbelievers) would not be able to perceive Him, because they could not see Him

(John 14:17). However, His followers would be able to fellowship with Him through the ministry of the Holy Spirit even though they could not physically see Him.

This was a promise from Jesus that just as His body would be resurrected, so ours will be also.

John 14:20

> *At that day ye shall know that I* am *in my Father, and ye in me, and I in you.*

In the New Covenant we have the indwelling presence of the Holy Spirit that assures us of God's presence with us (2 Cor. 5:5; 1 John 3:24 and 4:13). Praise God for giving us the Holy Spirit.

John 14:21

> *He that hath my commandments, and keepeth them, he it is that loveth me: and he that loveth me shall be loved of my Father, and I will love him, and will manifest myself to him.*

The English word *manifest* means "clearly apparent to the sight or understanding; obvious."[6] The Greek word *emphanizo*, from which "*manifest*" was translated here, means "to exhibit ... or disclose."[7] When we love the Lord in truth so that our actions bear that out, Jesus will manifest Himself to us. It will be clearly apparent to our sight or understanding. A failure to have Jesus revealed to us is a declaration that we don't really love Him the way we should.

It's very important to note that loving Jesus isn't revealed in us keeping the Old Testament Law. That was an oppressive set of commands that no one could keep. Jesus said that those who truly love Him would keep His commands. What were His commands? First John 3:23 says, "*And this is his commandment, That we should believe on the name of his Son Jesus Christ, and love one another, as he gave us commandment.*"

John 13:34 says, "*A new commandment I give unto you, That ye love one another; as I have loved you, that ye also love one another.*"

Keeping the commandments doesn't make us love God or make God love us. But loving God will make us keep the commandments.

Once again, this verse has been misinterpreted to say that keeping God's commandments will produce a love for God, but this verse is saying just the opposite. Loving God will produce keeping His commandments (see notes at John 14:15).

John 14:22

> *Judas saith unto him, not Iscariot, Lord, how is it that thou wilt manifest thyself unto us, and not unto the world?*

The Judas who asked this question wasn't Judas Iscariot, the betrayer (Luke 6:16).

Judas wasn't rebuked for his question the way Philip and Thomas had been earlier in this chapter. That's because Judas's question wasn't a question of unbelief but rather a question of *how* for the purpose of clarification. If we believe God's Word, it's never wrong to ask for clarification about what it means or how we can bring those promises to pass (Luke 1:34).

Judas asked a question, and Jesus replied without the rebuke that characterized His answers to Thomas and Philip in this same discourse (see notes at John 14:4 and John 14:7). This was because Judas's question was not a question of doubt, as were Thomas's and Philip's; Judas was simply seeking clarification of how this would be. Mary asked a similar question without being rebuked by the angel Gabriel (Luke 1:34). Therefore, we see that God doesn't mind us questioning Him if our motives are right.

John 14:23

Jesus answered and said unto him, If a man love me, he will keep my words: and my Father will love him, and we will come unto him, and make our abode with him.

Loving God makes us keep His words, not the other way around. Some people think that if they do what's right, then the Lord will love them in return; they are missing the great truth that Jesus was presenting here. That's spiritual dyslexia (1 John 2:5).

John 14:24

> *He that loveth me not keepeth not my sayings: and the word which ye hear is not mine, but the Father's which sent me.*

This statement causes many people to want to keep Jesus' sayings so that they can love God and receive these benefits. But that's the opposite of what Jesus was saying. Keeping Jesus' commandments doesn't make us love God; loving God will make us keep Jesus' commandments. This is a very important difference. Mixing this up is spiritual dyslexia (John 14:15 and 1 John 2:5).

John 14:25

> *These things have I spoken unto you, being* yet *present with you.*

I imagine that all of us would have loved to have been one of Jesus' disciples and to have heard Him speak these words firsthand. But Jesus revealed in John 16:7 that it is actually more advantageous to have the Holy Spirit speak to us than to hear Jesus' words in person. See my notes at John 16:7.

John 14:26

But the Comforter, which is *the Holy Ghost, whom the Father will send in my name, he shall teach you all things, and bring all things to your remembrance, whatsoever I have said unto you.*

The Holy Spirit is sent to teach us *all* things and bring *all* things to our remembrance that Jesus has spoken to us. There is no revelation knowledge apart from the enlightening power of the Holy Spirit.

The Holy Spirit is referred to as the "*Comforter*" four times in this discourse from Jesus to His disciples the night before His crucifixion (this verse, and vv. 14:16, 15:26, and 16:7). Also see my note at John 14:17.

Two of the great differences between the Old Testament saints and the New Testament saints are the indwelling of the Holy Spirit and the quickened understanding that the Holy Spirit gives. Four times in this one discourse, Jesus mentioned the Holy Spirit as being the source of God's revelation (first, this verse; second, John 15:26; third, vv. 16:7–11; and fourth, vv. 16:13–15). See my notes at John 16:13.

One of the ministries of the Holy Spirit is to bring back to our remembrance all things that Jesus has spoken unto us. This is the best note-taking system available. Everything that Jesus speaks will be brought back to us, while anything that was from the flesh will not. This ministry of the Holy Spirit is available to all believers who have received the Holy Spirit, but it is not operable in all Spirit-filled believers. It must be appropriated by faith. With a promise like this, there is no reason for believers to ever confess that they just can't remember the Word of God or the truths it teaches.

John 14:27

> *Peace I leave with you, my peace I give unto you: not as the world giveth, give I unto you. Let not your heart be troubled, neither let it be afraid.*

Jesus gave us *His* peace as a gift. Jesus had a supernatural peace in the midst of storms (Matt. 14:23–32 and Mark 4:37–41).

Therefore, our hearts don't have to be troubled, regardless of what happens. Our peace isn't human or natural. It's Jesus' divine peace that acts as a guard for our hearts and minds (Phil. 4:7).

Notice that it's our responsibility not to let our hearts be troubled. It's God's peace that empowers us, but that peace and power are under our authority.

The Greek word that was translated "*afraid*" at the end of this verse is *deiliao*, which means "to be timid."[8] Timidity is fear.

Peace is something that can be given (Matt. 10:13 and Luke 10:5–6).

Jesus distinguished His peace from what the world calls peace. In the world's mentality, peace is the absence of problems. However, God's peace is not dependent on circumstances. It is dependent only on God Himself who is the same yesterday, today, and forever (Heb. 13:8). Christians can have great peace even in the midst of terrible problems because their faith is in God. "*Thou wilt keep* him *in perfect peace,* whose *mind* is *stayed* on thee: *because he trusteth in thee*" (Isaiah 26:3).

As in John 14:1, "you" is the understood subject of this sentence, "*Let not your heart be troubled, neither let it be afraid.*" That means that the responsibility of not letting our hearts be troubled is ours. Jesus has given us His peace, but we have to receive it by faith to keep our hearts from being troubled.

Most people identify with fear in certain situations and think it only normal. However, God did not give us the spirit of fear (2 Tim. 1:7), and Jesus' command here shows that we have the power to reject fear.

John 14:28

Ye have heard how I said unto you, I go away, and come again *unto you. If ye loved me, ye would rejoice, because I said, I go unto the Father: for my Father is greater than I.*

What a powerful revelation! Jesus was speaking of His death. If Jesus' disciples loved Him more than they loved themselves, they would rejoice at His death. How is that?

Jesus had suffered criticism and rejection in this world as no one else ever has. Jesus also spoke constantly of longing to go to His Father. So, if the disciples had been thinking only of Jesus, they could have actually rejoiced at His death, because at least Jesus would then be at peace with His Father.

But the disciples weren't thinking about the welfare of Jesus. They were selfish; they were thinking about themselves. What would happen to them if Jesus was killed? They had thought that Jesus would establish His earthly kingdom and that they would rule with Him. What would they do? Where would they go? Their sorrow was all about them.

Self-centeredness is the root of all grief (Prov. 13:10). When we grieve at the death of loved ones who knew Jesus, our grief is all about us. Those believers who died are infinitely better off. Our sorrow is because we miss them. They don't miss us. They are in the presence of Jesus. Nothing could compete with that.

Jesus was saying that if the disciples were thinking of Him more than they were thinking of themselves, they would be happy that Jesus was returning to the Father. This is always the case when believers are taken from us in death. There is no reason to sorrow for those who are gone; they are blessed beyond measure. Our sorrow is really for ourselves.

Even from a selfish standpoint, the disciples had no reason to grieve because Jesus would return to them through the indwelling of the Holy Spirit. As He explained in the next few minutes, it was actually more advantageous to the disciples for Jesus to leave and send back the Holy Spirit (see my notes at John 16:7).

Jesus had already stated His union with the Father so clearly that He had been accused of blasphemy more than once (John 10:30). This statement about the Father being greater than Jesus must harmonize—not contradict—these other claims.

A key to understanding this is given in Philippians 2:6–8 where Paul stated that Jesus didn't think it robbery to be equal with God but humbled Himself, taking on the form of a servant (speaking of His humanity). Jesus was equal to God in His divine nature, but He made Himself inferior to the Father in regard to His humanity. Jesus didn't lose any of His deity when He became a man, but He did clothe it in flesh and submitted to the consequent limitations. In this sense, the Father was greater than Jesus.

John 14:29

> *And now I have told you before it come to pass, that, when it is come to pass, ye might believe.*

The fulfillment of prophecy is one of the strongest faith builders there is (Matt. 26:24).

A prophetic utterance is given for edification, exhortation, and comfort (1 Cor. 14:3). As Jesus revealed here, it also causes faith in the Lord when the prophecy comes to pass.

John 14:30

Hereafter I will not talk much with you: for the prince of this world cometh, and hath nothing in me.

Jesus knew there was going to be another major battle with the devil. Therefore, He wasn't going to speak much. "*In the multitude of words there wanteth not sin: but he that refraineth his lips* is *wise*" (Prov. 10:19).

If Jesus thought it wise to refrain His words when confronting the devil, then how much more should we do the same?

"*The prince of this world*" is referring to Satan (Matt. 4:9 and Luke 4:4). Satan is also called the prince of this world in John 12:31 and 16:11.

"*Hath nothing in me*" is a reference to the fact that there was no sin or weakness in Jesus that Satan could take advantage of. Satan had no right to kill Jesus. Jesus gave His life for us (John 6:51 and 10:17–18).

John 14:31

But that the world may know that I love the Father; and as the Father gave me commandment, even so I do. Arise, let us go hence.

Jesus knew He was marching straight into His own death. Nevertheless, He faced the torture willingly because it would glorify His Father. Jesus was totally unselfish. What a contrast with fallen humanity. We can see through Jesus that this selflessness is the way the Lord created us to be. How far we have fallen!

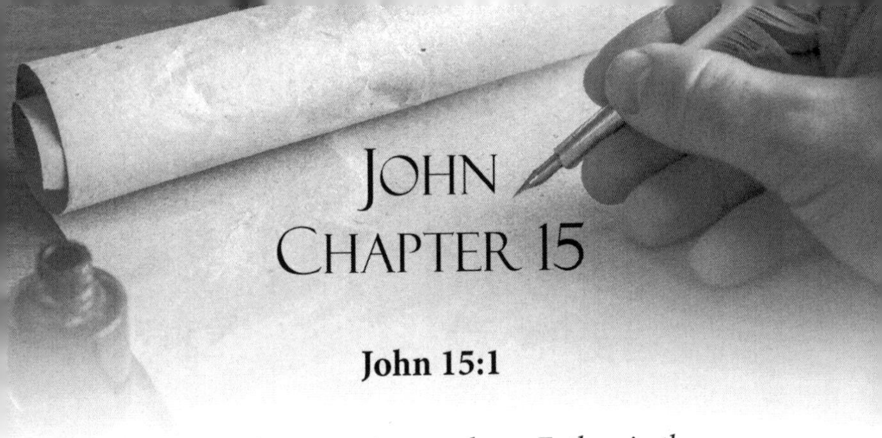

John Chapter 15

John 15:1

I am the true vine, and my Father is the husbandman.

Each one of us is attached to a vine of some sort. If it's not the true Vine (Jesus), then it's some other vine that ultimately is part of Satan's kingdom. There is no such thing as a self-made man or woman. Either God or the devil is flowing their life or death through us.

This parable repeats a familiar theme of growth common to many of Jesus' teachings (Matt. 13:31 and Mark 4:31). John 15:2 speaks of "*fruit*," then "*more fruit*," and finally in John 15:5 and 8, "*much fruit*." There is no shortcut to bearing much fruit. We must grow (1 Pet. 2:2).

John 15:2

> *Every branch in me that beareth not fruit he taketh away: and every* branch *that beareth fruit, he purgeth it, that it may bring forth more fruit.*

What is this fruit that Jesus was speaking of? Some have taken a very narrow interpretation to say that it is producing another Christian, and therefore any believers who don't reproduce their faith will be taken away. That cannot be verified by other scriptures.

This fruit could be referring to many things. Paul spoke of the fruit of the Spirit (Gal. 5:22–23), the fruits of righteousness (Phil. 1:11), new converts as fruit (Rom. 1:13), and holiness as a fruit (Rom. 6:22). Jesus could have been speaking of any one or any combination of these things. It is most probable that He was simply using the word "fruit" to denote any of the virtues that God's Word advocates.

This purging has been interpreted in many ways. The illustration that Jesus was using is one of pruning; therefore, some have said this purging is a very painful process where the Lord cuts and slashes us through things like sickness, death, poverty, and other forms of tragedy so that eventually we will bear more fruit. This teaching promotes problems not only as a good thing but also as a necessity if we want to bear more fruit. That thinking is not consistent with the rest of God's Word or even the context of this verse.

The Greek word used for "*purgeth*" in this verse is *kathairo*, and it means "to cleanse."[9] In John 15:3, the Greek word translated "clean" is *katharos*, which is akin to *kathairo*. *Katharos* means to "free from impure admixture."[10] The text makes it very clear that the purging Jesus spoke of is done through the word that He has spoken unto us (John 15:3).

Paul said in 2 Timothy 3:16–17 that, "*All scripture* is *given by inspiration of God, and* is *profitable for doctrine, for reproof, for correction, for instruction in righteousness: that the man of God may be perfect, throughly furnished unto all good works.*"

That is God's method of pruning us, and He doesn't need the devil's help. His Word will make us "*perfect, throughly furnished unto all good works.*" That is not to say that we cannot learn through tragedy. We can. But God has a better way. If we mistakenly think that God is bringing tragedy into our lives to make us more fruitful, then we'll not resist the tragedies, and they will not flee from us (James 4:7). All of us will learn by hard knocks, but those who welcome that with their arms open wide will suffer greatly and be far behind those who let God's Word have its perfect work in them.

John 15:3

> *Now ye are clean through the word which I have spoken unto you.*

Purge can be defined as "to cleanse." Indeed, the Greek word *katharos*, which was translated "*clean*" in this verse, is simply the adjective form of the Greek word *kathairo*, which was translated "*purgeth*" in the previous verse (v. 15:2).[11]

Here Jesus told how this purging, or cleansing, will take place. It comes through His Word. God doesn't purge, or cleanse, us with problems. His Word is given to discipline, correct, and make us thoroughly furnished unto every good work (2 Tim. 3:16–17).

John 15:4

Abide in me, and I in you. As the branch cannot bear fruit of itself, except it abide in the vine; no more can ye, except ye abide in me.

The Greek word meno that was translated "*abide*" in this verse, means "to stay (in a given place, state, relation, or expectancy)."[12] The *American Heritage Dictionary* defines *abide* as "to remain in a place...to dwell or reside."[13] Every definition, whether in Greek or English, stresses some point of consistency. We cannot claim to abide in Jesus if we only have communion with Him occasionally. Abiding in Jesus involves constant communion with the Lord. The just live by faith (Hab. 2:4, Rom. 1:17, Gal. 3:11, and Heb. 10:38); they don't just visit there occasionally.

The word "*abide*" stresses consistency. Going through spells where we really seek God will not substitute for abiding in God. This is one major reason why more Christians don't experience the abundant life that Jesus came to bring (John 10:10). Most people only really abide in Jesus when the going gets tough. Then when the pressure lets up, they relax and go back to doing their own thing, and that hastens the next crisis.

This is a very profound truth that is the key to bearing fruit, but it is so easy to forget. Because the fruit is borne on the branch, it is easy to credit the branch with the fruit, when it is the vine that drew the life from the earth and channeled it through the branch. Likewise, since we are the branches through which the life of God flows, we sometimes think that it is our own holiness that produces the fruit. The moment we think that way, we are no longer abiding (trusting in, clinging to) in the vine, and we will become fruitless if we persist in that mindset.

This is actually a great relief if we understand this and apply it properly. It puts all the responsibility on Jesus. Our only responsibility is to respond to His ability. Just like we have never seen a branch travailing to bring forth fruit, all we have to do is labor to rest (trust and depend) completely on Jesus as our source (Heb. 4:11). If we abide in Him, fruit is natural.

John 15:5

I am the vine, ye are *the branches: He that abideth in me, and I in him, the same bringeth forth much fruit: for without me ye can do nothing.*

Most Christians know they need to abide in the Lord more, but they don't feel they have the time. If we would see ourselves as worthless as a detached branch without Jesus, we would make the time. The more demands we have on us, the more we need to abide in the Lord.

Abiding in the Lord certainly demands intimacy that cannot be achieved without time spent alone with the Lord. But we must also learn to be in communion with the Lord during our daily activities. It is unrealistic and not God's will for us to try to live lives of total seclusion. But we can bring every thought under the control and into subjection to the mind of Christ (2 Cor. 10:3–5).

These verses parallel Psalms 91:1, where the Lord promises divine blessing and intervention to those who *dwell* in the secret place of the Almighty. As a branch cannot just abide in the vine for fifteen minutes at a time, so we can't think a fifteen-minute devotional is the same as abiding in the vine. We can't just visit the Lord. We have to dwell in His presence.

It is absolutely true that without Jesus, we can do nothing. But it is also absolutely true that we are never without Him (Matt. 28:20 and Heb. 13:5). There needs to be a balance here. We need to recognize our total dependence on Him but not so focused on our inability that we forget we can do all things through Him (Phil. 4:13).

John 15:6

> *If a man abide not in me, he is cast forth as a branch, and is withered; and men gather them, and cast* them *into the fire, and they are burned.*

Our failures are a result of not abiding in Christ, the Vine. In the illustration the Apostle Paul gave in 1 Corinthians 3:10–15, true believers will still be saved even though their works of the flesh will be burned, and they will suffer loss.

Notice that Jesus didn't say *He* would cast forth the unfruitful branches. God is not the one who punishes His true believers (John 12:32 and Rom. 8:28). But when we unplug from the source of all our strength and blessings (i.e., God), we do become unfruitful, for we can do nothing without Him (John 15:5). People will devour us when we are living out of our own strength. We must abide in the Vine.

John 15:7

If ye abide in me, and my words abide in you, ye shall ask what ye will, and it shall be done unto you.

Everyone wants to get whatever they pray for (see my note at John 14:13), but very few are willing to abide in Jesus. This promise is conditional on our abiding. It's not God who fails to answer our prayers if we aren't abiding in Him. Instead, it is Satan who hinders our prayers when we aren't abiding in Jesus, and our carnality that results from our *non*-abiding life renders us powerless to do anything about it.

This is not a promise that if we meet certain conditions, the Lord will grant any request, even if it doesn't line up with

His Word. When we are abiding in Jesus and His words are abiding in us, our desires change. This is not promising that God will change to accommodate us, but rather, this is a statement that we will change to accommodate God.

John 15:8

Herein is my Father glorified, that ye bear much fruit; so shall ye be my disciples.

A true disciple of Jesus is one who bears much fruit (see my notes at John 15:1). Those who are not bearing much fruit are not yet disciples. In John 8:31–32, Jesus said, "*If ye continue in my word,* then *are ye my disciples indeed; And ye shall know the truth, and the truth shall make you free.*"

It could be said that when we come to really know the truth, the freedom we experience bears much fruit, and we become disciples indeed.

Discipleship should be the aim of every Christian. Sadly, the commission Jesus gave in Matthew 28:19–20 has changed from making disciples to making converts who only ask the Lord for forgiveness of sins so that they can avoid hell. They aren't focused on becoming true followers of Jesus; they just want "fire insurance." That is not what being a Christian was intended to be.

Some people have ignored this scripture in an effort to justify their failures. They proclaim that God willed them not to succeed so that they would be humble or some such foolishness. However, this verse settles, once and for all, that barrenness doesn't glorify God, but fruitfulness does. It is God's will for us to have the fruit that God's Word promises.

The word *disciple* means a learner of or follower of. If the disciples bear much fruit, then they will truly be following the example of Jesus who saw everything that the Father gave Him to do come to fruition.

John 15:9

As the Father hath loved me, so have I loved you: continue ye in my love.

Jesus loves us just as much as God the Father loves Jesus. That's amazing! He doesn't change; He's always the same

(Heb. 13:8). So, His love for us doesn't change. Yet we have to remain in His love. He doesn't stop loving; we stop remaining.

In the first part of this chapter, Jesus stressed how we have to abide in Him as a branch abides in the vine in order to be fruitful. This statement about continuing in His love is making the same point. Abiding in Jesus and continuing in His love are the same thing (1 John 4:16).

This is an amazing statement. Jesus was worthy of all the love given unto Him by His Father, but we aren't. How could Jesus love us with the same love that His Father had for Him? This is because God's love is unconditional and isn't given based on our performance. It goes beyond our ability to understand it, but we can accept it through faith (1 John 3:1–2).

Jesus continues loving us because His love wasn't based on our performance in the first place. But we can refuse His love, or else Jesus would not have told us to continue in His love (see notes at John 15:10).

John 15:10

If ye keep my commandments, ye shall abide in my love; even as I have kept my Father's commandments, and abide in his love.

Keeping Jesus' commandments doesn't affect God loving us. But it affects us loving God. Therefore, keeping Jesus' commandments keeps us in His love. It doesn't affect His loving but our remaining.

This is illustrated in God's relationship with Adam and Eve. God gave them a commandment not to eat of the Tree of the Knowledge of Good and Evil (Gen. 2:17). The Lord loved them before He gave the commandment, and He loved them even after they violated His command, as can be seen in Him making them clothes to cover their nakedness (Gen. 3:21) and giving them a promise of redemption (Gen. 3:15). But they departed from God's love through breaking His command, and it cost them dearly (Rom. 6:23a).

Therefore, if they had kept the Lord's commandment, they would have remained in His love.

God's love was commended toward us while we were yet sinners (Rom. 5:8). We certainly weren't keeping the commandments of God then. Therefore, keeping the commandments doesn't affect God's willingness to love us, but it does affect our awareness of how much God loves us.

If we live in sin, our consciences become defiled and condemn us (Rom. 2:15). That's not God condemning us (Rom. 8:1 and 34) but our consciences. God still loves us (Rom. 8:35–39). John was speaking of this same thing in 1 John 3:20 when he said, "*For if our heart condemn us, God is greater than our heart, and knoweth all things.*"

However, as far as this earthly life goes, our awareness of God's love is everything. Therefore, we must keep Satan from blinding us to the love of God. The most effective way of doing this is to give no place to the devil through sin (Rom. 6:16).

John went on to say in 1 John 3:21, "*Beloved, if our heart condemn us not,* then *have we confidence toward God.*"

Holiness is very important in keeping our hearts assured of the love of God (1 John 3:19), and this is what Jesus was referring to.

John 15:11

These things have I spoken unto you, that my joy might remain in you, and that *your joy might be full.*

Our flesh always sees abiding in Jesus as something that takes away all our fun. Yet Jesus said that abiding in Him would cause us to have fullness of joy. There is a depth of joy and satisfaction from abiding in Jesus that nothing this world has to offer can match. Those who don't have this joy that Jesus was speaking of aren't abiding in Him. That's it. There is no other reason. In the presence of the Lord, there is fullness of joy (Ps. 16:11). If we are truly believing, we will rejoice with joy unspeakable and full of glory (1 Pet. 1:8).

These statements about keeping Jesus' commandments were spoken not to bring oppression but rather that the joy of the Lord might abound in us. It is the devil's oldest trick to tell us that the commandments of God are given to keep us from being happy. That's the line he sold Eve (Gen. 3:4–5). Choosing her own way over God's way surely didn't bring Eve happiness. God has given us commandments because

He wants us to be happy, and we don't have enough sense on our own to pick the right way (Prov. 16:25 and Jer. 10:23); therefore, He chose for us. If we will keep the Lord's commandments, this will assure us that our joy will be full.

The Lord desires for us to have joy—and not just joy but fullness of joy. Christians are the only ones who really have anything to be happy about. Remember that Jesus was saying all these things in John 14–15 so that we would not be offended in trying times (John 16:1, see notes at John 14:2).

Joy is one of the strongest weapons we have against depression and discouragement. It is an offensive weapon against the devil (Matt. 4:9 and 21:16). In a situation where our faith is being severely tested, praise to the Lord will take our attention away from our problems and focus it on Jesus, thereby releasing the joy that comes through faith (1 Pet. 1:8).

John 15:12

This is my commandment, That ye love one another, as I have loved you.

The commandment of Jesus isn't rules and regulations. It's just loving one another (John 13:34). This is repeating what Jesus said to His disciples earlier in the evening (John 13:34). Those who abide in love abide in God (1 John 4:16), for God is love (1 John 4:8 and 16).

This command for us to love each other as Christ has loved us is greater than the Old Testament command to love our neighbor as ourselves (Lev. 19:18).

Notice that Jesus said that love was His commandment (singular). There were other commandments that He gave, but just as He summed up all the Old Testament commandments into two (Matt. 22:36), so all His New Testament commandments can be summed up into one commandment of love for God and our fellow man.

Some people put Jesus in a totally different class than themselves, thereby excusing themselves from following His example because, after all, they aren't Jesus. It's true that in ourselves, none of us are like Jesus, but it is also true that it is not us living this Christian life but Christ living in us (Gal.

2:20). Therefore, our goals should be no less than the perfect standard that Jesus set for us.

John 15:13

Greater love hath no man than this, that a man lay down his life for his friends.

God's kind of love is characterized by putting others ahead of self (Phil. 2:3). The greatest expression of self-sacrifice for others is laying down one's life. Yet it has to be done from the proper motive (1 Cor. 13:3).

Some have perverted the love Jesus was speaking about to apply it in a way that is inconsistent with Jesus' own actions. For instance, Jesus made a whip and drove the money changers out of the temple twice (John 2:13–16 and Mark 11:15–17). He called people names (Luke 13:32 and Matt. 23:13–33). He pronounced judgment upon those who refused His ministry (Matt. 11:21 and Luke 10:13). See Matthew 22:39.

Jesus was stating to what degree we should carry out this command to love one another. We should follow Jesus' example and go all the way to laying down our lives for one another.

John 15:14

Ye are my friends, if ye do whatsoever I command you.

The previous verse says that laying down our lives for our friends is the greatest expression of love. Here, Jesus said that He is our friend—because He was laying down His life for us and because we are His friends when we lay down our lives for Him.

What an honor to be called the friend of God. Only one man prior to this time was ever called the friend of God: Abraham (2 Chr. 20:7, Is. 41:8, and James 2:23). Now this is the true title of all who believe on Jesus.

Keeping the Lord's commands doesn't make us His friends. But if we are His friends, we will keep His commandments (1 John 2:3–5).

Abraham was referred to as the friend of God (2 Chr. 20:7, Is. 41:8, and James 2:23). The Scriptures state that God spoke to Moses as friend speaks to friend (Exod. 33:11). Here, this rare relationship with God was being opened up to all who would do whatsoever Jesus commands them.

It is wonderful that we can have any relationship with Almighty God at all, but a relationship as a friend is beyond anything that we could ask or think.

As Jesus went on to explain in John 15:15, one of the benefits of this friendship is that we get information to which no one else has access. This was also true of Abraham, the friend of God (Gen. 18:17–22).

John 15:15

Henceforth I call you not servants; for the servant knoweth not what his lord doeth: but I have called you friends; for all things that I have heard of my Father I have made known unto you.

Paul called himself a voluntary servant, or slave, of Christ (Rom. 1:1, Phil. 1:1, and Titus 1:1). Paul also said that believers are no longer servants but sons of God and heirs with Christ (Gal. 4:7).

But the word "*friend*" denotes an intimacy with Christ that was rare under the Old Covenant (see my note at John 15:14). Friends know each other much better than slaves and masters know each other. We are now friends of God. Thank You, Jesus!

John 15:16

> *Ye have not chosen me, but I have chosen you, and ordained you, that ye should go and bring forth fruit, and* that *your fruit should remain: that whatsoever ye shall ask of the Father in my name, he may give it you.*

People will often say that they found the Lord. But the truth is that the Lord found us. He wasn't lost; we were. We can't come to the Lord unless His Holy Spirit draws us: "*No man can come to me, except the Father which hath sent me draw him: and I will raise him up at the last day* (John 6:44).

The Lord didn't choose us for failure but for success. His will is that each one of us bear much fruit (see my notes at John 15:1) that lasts. We aren't supposed to just make converts but disciples who will continue in God's Word. John 8:31–32 says, "*Then said Jesus to those Jews which believed on him, If ye continue in my word,* then *are ye my disciples indeed; And ye shall know the truth, and the truth shall make you free.*"

We didn't find God; He found us. God wasn't lost; we were. It is God who draws us to Himself (John 6:44), gives us the faith to believe (Eph. 2:8), and works His pleasure in us (Phil. 2:13). Remembering our debt (Rom. 1:14) will motivate us to bring forth fruit.

We all have a God-given purpose in this life—to bring forth fruit. Just as a person plants a tree and expects to reap fruit from it, God expects fruit from us (Luke 13:6–9).

Notice not only that Jesus ordained us to bring forth fruit but also that our fruit should remain. Many times we

Christians, in our zeal to bring forth fruit, aren't too concerned with whether it lasts or not. That is not the way God feels. Only the fruit that lasts will receive the Lord's stamp of approval. No doubt His statistics will vary greatly from ours.

John 15:17

These things I command you, that ye love one another.

This is Jesus' commandment (John 13:34 and 15:12). Jesus said that the greatest commandment in all of the Old Testament was to love God with all of our hearts, souls, minds, and strength (Mark 12:30). Then He said that the second greatest commandment was to love our neighbors as ourselves (Mark 12:31). All of the Old Testament Law was summed up in these two commands (Matt. 22:36–40 and Rom. 13:8–10).

The Lord reduced this even further to this one law, to love one another as He loved us (John 13:34). We can only love others if we first love God and receive His love for us. So, loving others includes loving God. We can't give away what we haven't received.

John 15:18

If the world hate you, ye know that it hated me before it hated *you.*

If we are persecuted for our Christian witness, we don't need to feel like we are alone. Jesus suffered infinitely more than any of us have (Heb. 12:3–5). He knows exactly how we feel (Heb. 2:17–18) and can help us in our times of need (Heb. 4:15–16).

Satan will often try to use persecution or affliction to bring us into self-pity. It always helps to recognize that our problems aren't unique. Peter shared that afflictions are common to all believers (1 Pet. 5:9) in an effort to encourage the saints, and here Jesus was employing this same truth to keep His disciples from being offended (John 16:1).

John 15:19

If ye were of the world, the world would love his own: but because ye are not of the

> *world, but I have chosen you out of the world, therefore the world hateth you.*

If we really believe what Jesus was saying here, we shouldn't be surprised when we are persecuted. It should be just the opposite. We should be surprised if we aren't persecuted. As the Apostle Paul said in 2 Timothy 3:12, "*All that will live godly in Christ Jesus shall suffer persecution.*" The only Christians who aren't persecuted are ungodly ones.

No truly godly person will be embraced by those who hate God. They might be known by the godly, but they won't be loved by the ungodly.

We should not think it is strange to be persecuted (1 Pet. 4:12). "*Yea, and all that will live godly in Christ Jesus shall suffer persecution*" (2 Tim. 3:12).

We can actually rejoice because we are being persecuted for Jesus' sake (Acts 5:41), knowing that the Lord will be with us in the midst of the persecution (1 Pet. 4:13–14) and that there will be more than ample reward when we stand before Him (Heb. 11:26). For more information on persecution, see Matthew 5:10 and Luke 8:14.

Persecution is a token that those doing the persecuting are under conviction. They realize that they are not living what your words or actions are advocating. So, in defense of self, they attack the one whom they perceive to be the source of their conviction. If this is understood, it makes persecution much easier to take. They aren't just mad at you; they are convicted. When the Gospel is presented in the power of the Holy Spirit, there will always be either revival or riot but not indifference.

John 15:20

> *Remember the word that I said unto you, The servant is not greater than his lord. If they have persecuted me, they will also persecute you; if they have kept my saying, they will keep yours also.*

Jesus had said this to His disciples before in Matthew 10:24, Luke 6:40, and John 13:16.

It is often frustrating for me to see people reject my ministry, but it really helps to remember that, as a whole, the people rejected Jesus too. I shouldn't expect to be treated better than Jesus.

Proverbs 13:12 says, "*Hope deferred maketh the heart sick.*" If believers have the mistaken opinion that they will not suffer persecution, then their hearts will be sick quite often. Jesus was preparing His disciples for the inevitable so that they would not be offended when it came (John 16:1–4).

In the midst of persecution, Satan will try to convince us that this strife is all our fault. If he succeeds, then we back down, and the pressure is off his followers. However, Jesus suffered continual rejection and persecution, yet we know that the problem was not with Him but with those who rejected Him. Jesus was making it clear that persecution is an inevitable part of a godly life (2 Tim. 3:12) so that we will not fall prey to introspection and self-condemnation when rejection comes. If our sinless Savior was rejected, then certainly we will be too.

John 15:21

But all these things will they do unto you for my name's sake, because they know not him that sent me.

People who don't love the Lord won't love us either if we are living like the Lord. The same things they hate in the Lord they will hate in us. The only Christians this isn't true of are those who aren't living godly lives (2 Tim. 3:12).

John 15:22

If I had not come and spoken unto them, they had not had sin: but now they have no cloke for their sin.

Those who have received greater revelation are more accountable than others (Luke 12:48). Therefore, those who saw, heard, and rejected Jesus are more accountable than others who rejected God. They have no excuse. Jesus was a perfect representation of God the Father (Heb. 1:3), yet the majority of those who heard Him rejected His message.

Speaking the truth of God's Word removes the "*cloke*" [cloak] people use to hide sin. When exposed, they rebel at the messenger because their evil deeds are revealed (John 3:19–20).

Jesus was not saying that those who had rejected Him had no sin. The Scriptures say that "*all have sinned*" (Rom. 3:23) and "*There is none righteous, no, not one*" (Rom. 3:10). This very verse shows that Jesus didn't cause them to sin but simply removed the cloak that they were hiding their sin behind.

In John 15:21, Jesus said that they didn't know the Father. In John 15:23, He said, "*He that hateth me hateth my Father also*." The Jews, of whom He was speaking, already had the sin of unbelief in their hearts, but they were covering it over with their pious acts. When Jesus came revealing the sins of the heart, their cover was blown, and their sin appeared in their hatred and rejection of Jesus.

Jesus was saying these things in reference to persecution, and, as He went on to say in John 15:25, this persecution came through no fault of His. The purpose of these statements was to warn His disciples against feeling guilty or condemned when persecution came. The Word strips people of the disguises they have been hiding their sins behind, and persecution is a natural result.

John 15:23

He that hateth me hateth my Father also.

Many people who hated Jesus claimed that they were totally devoted to God. That just wasn't true. The true worshipers of God loved Jesus, His Son. Likewise today, there are people who claim to love God but don't acknowledge Jesus as the only way to the Father (John 14:6). They are also liars.

Multitudes of people embrace religion and its rituals and Christian trappings, but they aren't in fellowship with the Father. If they were truly in fellowship with God, He would lead them to His Son, Jesus. Regardless of their words, those who hate Jesus hate the true and living God too.

This is one more verse in a growing list of scriptures where Jesus equated any form of rejection of Him or who He claimed to be as a rejection of God the Father (John 5:23

and 10:30). Any group who claims to have access to God the Father without exalting Jesus to an equal position is completely deceived.

John 15:24

> *If I had not done among them the works which none other man did, they had not had sin: but now have they both seen and hated both me and my Father.*

Jesus was the express image of God the Father (Heb. 1:3). The works that He did testified of who He was in such a clear way that any rational soul would have believed on Him (John 5:36–37 and 10:37–38). Those who saw the miracles of Jesus yet didn't believe don't have any excuse.

John 15:25

> *But* this cometh to pass, *that the word might be fulfilled that is written in their law, They hated me without a cause.*

This is a quotation from Psalm 69:4. There is a similar passage in Psalm 109:3. No one is ever justified in hating Jesus, either back then when He walked on the earth, or now.

John 15:26

But when the Comforter is come, whom I will send unto you from the Father, even *the Spirit of truth, which proceedeth from the Father, he shall testify of me:*

Four times in this discourse that Jesus gave to His disciples the night before His crucifixion, He called the Holy Spirit the "*Comforter*" (this verse, and vv. 14:16, 14:26, and 16:7). This is a descriptive title depicting the ministry of the Holy Spirit. Religion today has portrayed Him more as an accuser or condemner, but that's not accurate. He is a Comforter, just like Jesus (see my notes at John 14:16 and John 16:8–11).

John 15:27

And ye also shall bear witness, because ye have been with me from the beginning.

John 15:26 speaks of the Holy Spirit testifying of Jesus. Here, Jesus said we also will bear witness. Indeed, it is the Holy Spirit speaking through us when we witness (Mark 13:11).

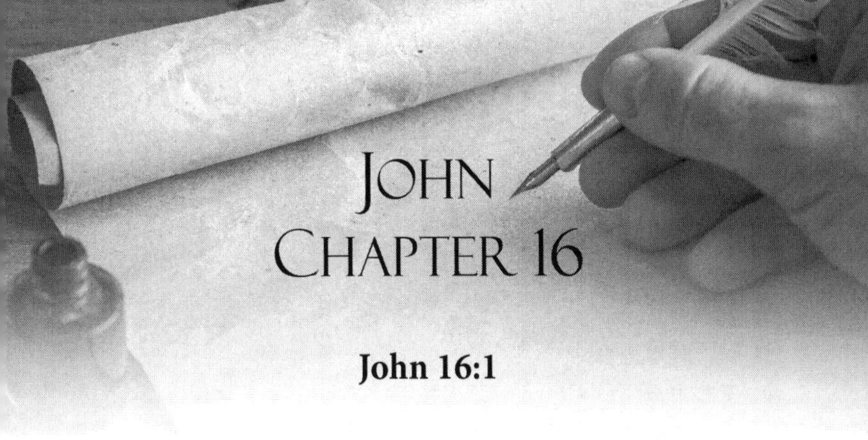

John Chapter 16

John 16:1

These things have I spoken unto you, that ye should not be offended.

Jesus was speaking these things to His disciples the night before His crucifixion. He was preparing them for the worst time of their lives. Yet if they had taken heed to His instructions, they wouldn't have been offended, even during the crucifixion and the three days before Jesus was resurrected. If Jesus' words could sustain a person through that, then there is no excuse for us not being able to bear up under our problems.

Jesus clearly stated that He told His disciples these things so that they wouldn't be offended, yet He prophesied in Matthew 26:31 and Mark 14:27 that they would all be offended because of Him that night. That means that this didn't have to happen, but Jesus knew that it would. He didn't cause them to be offended, but He knew how they would respond to the night's events.

This also illustrates that even though Jesus knew they would be offended, He spoke what they needed to know to not be offended. Jesus didn't withhold the truth from them, even though He knew that they would not heed it. This is how we should deal with people. We don't have the right to reject truth for others. We should speak the truth in love (Eph. 4:15) and give them the right to accept it or reject it on their own. If we withhold the truth because we don't think that they will receive, we reject the truth for them. That's not what Jesus did.

John 16:2

> *They shall put you out of the synagogues: yea, the time cometh, that whosoever killeth you will think that he doeth God service.*

Is this a prophecy that applies to Jesus' twelve disciples only? As Jesus spoke of the end times in Matthew 10:17–22, Mark 13:9–13, and Luke 21:12–19, He made it very clear that His disciples would be hated by *all* men. Therefore, this prophecy is for all Christians in all lands. All those who live godly in

Christ Jesus shall suffer persecution (2 Tim. 3:12). The only "Christians" who aren't persecuted are ungodly "Christians."

John 16:3

> *And these things will they do unto you, because they have not known the Father, nor me.*

What a statement! Those who persecute true believers testify to all who have ears to hear and eyes to see that they are not true Christians.

John 16:4

> *But these things have I told you, that when the time shall come, ye may remember that I told you of them. And these things I said not unto you at the beginning, because I was with you.*

As long as Jesus was with the disciples, He was the focus of the Jews' persecution. Any rejection the disciples encountered by association was more than compensated for by the fact that Jesus was physically present to comfort and instruct them. All this was soon to change. After Jesus' ascension, the disciples encountered the full force of the Jews' rejection even to the point of martyrdom. Jesus assured them that His words about persecution would comfort them. He then went on to mention again the coming Holy Spirit and even stated that the comfort of the Holy Spirit would be even better because He would be in them (John 14:17 and 16:7).

John 16:5

> *But now I go my way to him that sent me; and none of you asketh me, Whither goest thou?*

The disciples had asked Jesus this very question just moments before (John 14:5), and their reaction in John 16:17–18 shows that they still didn't understand what Jesus was saying to them. They must have at least understood that Jesus was speaking of leaving them, and that's why sorrow had filled their hearts (John 16:6).

John 16:6

But because I have said these things unto you, sorrow hath filled your heart.

Jesus had spoken of His death and the ensuing persecution against His disciples. Most of us would think that this couldn't produce anything but sorrow. But if the disciples had fully understood what was happening, they could have rejoiced. The departure of Jesus and the indwelling of the Holy Spirit in each one of their hearts was better than having Jesus there in His physical body (John 16:7). What a revelation!

Many ministers today would never say anything that would cause sorrow to fill someone's heart. They are under the deception that all sermons should be uplifting and positive. While it is true that the Gospel is the best news ever presented, there are times when the truth will cause people grief (2 Cor. 7:9–11 and Gal. 4:16). Jesus' farewell address to His disciples caused sorrow to fill their hearts.

John 16:7

Nevertheless I tell you the truth; It is expedient for you that I go away: for if I

> *go not away, the Comforter will not come unto you; but if I depart, I will send him unto you.*

What an amazing statement! What could be better than having Jesus physically present with us? The answer is, having the Holy Spirit indwell us. When Jesus was in His physical body, He was limited to being in one place at one time. Therefore, He wasn't completely available to every believer all the time. But through the Holy Spirit, He now indwells each one of us and will never leave us nor forsake us (Heb. 13:5).

Also, Jesus' physical body was natural. It wasn't sinful, but it was plain (Is. 53:2). The disciples constantly missed who Jesus really was on the inside because they were so dominated by their senses. But now that we have the indwelling Holy Spirit, whose primary purpose is to reveal the true Jesus to us, we can know Jesus in a more intimate way and with more understanding than His first disciples knew Him. What a deal!

Jesus said that He would send the Holy Spirit to dwell with us when He went back to His Father (John 7:39 and 14:16–18). Therefore, the indwelling of the Holy Spirit in the life of the believer is proof that Jesus made it and is seated at the right hand of the Father.

Notice the terminology that Jesus used to describe the Holy Spirit. Jesus called Him the Comforter. See my note at John 15:26.

The Greek word translated "*expedient*" is *sumphero*, and it means "to be an advantage, profitable."[14] How could any situation be more advantageous or profitable than having Jesus physically with you?

When Jesus walked on this earth in His physical body, He was subject to many physical limitations. For instance, He could not always be with every one of His disciples all the time. Through the ministry of the Holy Spirit, He could. Instead of Satan getting rid of Jesus, 120 "little Christs" (that is literally what the word "Christian" means) came out of the Upper Room on the Day of Pentecost.

Jesus had taught His disciples as no teacher ever had, but they had very little understanding because they had not been born again yet (1 Cor. 2:14). However, when the Holy Spirit came, He would lead them into all truth (John 14:26 and 16:13) and even show them things to come (John 16:13).

The list of advantages of having the Holy Spirit in us, as compared to having Jesus with us in His physical body, goes on and on. The advantages can all be summed up in the fact that Jesus' power is now complete (Matt. 28:18) and no longer confined to one physical body.

John 16:8

And when he is come, he will reprove the world of sin, and of righteousness, and of judgment:

This is not a negative ministry as many people think. The Holy Spirit doesn't convict people of things they do that are wrong but of the fact that they aren't believing on Jesus (John 16:9).

Those who don't tithe or give will not be convicted about their lack of giving but about the fact that they aren't trusting Jesus with their finances. All acts of sin come from the one act of not believing on and resting in relationship with Jesus.

Adam and Eve's sin wasn't eating of the fruit, but not believing God's Word and the goodness of God. They bought the lie that God had withheld something good from them (Gen. 3:5). They doubted God and believed the devil. Eating the forbidden fruit was just the result of their unbelief.

David said, "*Against thee, thee only, have I sinned*" (Ps. 51:4). The Lord said to David in 2 Samuel 12:10 that when David committed adultery and murder, he had despised God. At its root, David's sin was really against God, not Uriah and Bathsheba.

Joseph kept his virginity because he told Potiphar's wife that he could not sin against God and do this great wickedness in His sight (Gen. 39:9).

The reason not to steal is because that action reveals a lack of trust in God as our source. The real reason not to commit adultery is because that act reveals that we do not believe the Lord when He said that from the beginning, God made them male and female and that the two are to become one flesh (Mark 10:6–8). We are not content with the one the Lord has given us, and we are not full of God's love. If we were, we would not be looking to someone else to fill that void.

The real temptation for Jesus was not to turn the stone into bread (Matt. 4:3), etc.; it was to disbelieve God. His Father had just told Him in an audible voice that He was His Son and that He was well pleased in Him (Matt. 3:17 and Luke 3:22). When Satan said, "If You are the Son of God," he was trying to get Jesus to establish His identity outside of what God said about Him (Matt. 4:3).

This is the same way he tries to tempt us today. The question most of us are asking is not the real question. Therefore, the answer we are getting is not the real answer.

Hebrews 4:15 says that Jesus was tempted in all points like as we are yet was without sin. Jesus wasn't tempted with cocaine. He was tempted with unbelief, though. That is the root of all sin, and Jesus endured that in all its facets.

There are just three main areas where Satan can tempt us with unbelief: the lust of the flesh, the lust of the eyes, and the pride of life (1 John 2:16). Jesus endured three temptations.

It is the ministry of the Holy Spirit to reprove of sin, righteousness, and judgment. It is not our ministry. We are simply witnesses (John 15:27 and Acts 1:8). Witnesses are not the judge or the jury. They simply testify of what they have seen or what has happened to them.

In their zeal, some people have gone beyond the witness stage and tried themselves to bring people under conviction. This is assuming a job that belongs to the Holy Spirit alone. This not only frustrates the witness, but it also drives many people away from God. We make a very poor Holy Spirit; therefore, we should stick to our job of being witnesses and let the Holy Spirit do His.

John 16:9

Of sin, because they believe not on me;

It is always an evil heart of unbelief that makes us depart from the living God (Heb. 3:12). Our actions are not the real problem; they are just the results and symptoms of our evil hearts of unbelief. That is what the Holy Spirit convicts us of.

People don't go to hell for their individual actions. The sins of the whole world have already been paid for (1 John 2:2). Individual sins are not the issue. The sin that sends people to hell is rejection of Jesus, and that is what the Holy Spirit convicts them of.

The Holy Spirit doesn't convict believers that they are going to hell for the rejection of Jesus. That is not the case. All of their sins are paid for—past, present, and even future sins (Rom. 4:8; Heb. 9:12, 14, 26, 28, 10:10 and 14). But the Holy Spirit will convict believers about their trust or lack of trust in Jesus. That's what it is all about: relationship.

If believers commit adultery, the Holy Spirit will speak to them about their lack of relationship with the Lord. Why aren't they satisfied with Jesus and the mate He has given them? That's exactly what the Lord spoke to David (2 Sam. 12:10).

Christians who are having problems with alcohol or drugs are actually having problems with trusting in Jesus. They are using some substance to cope instead of turning to Jesus.

The underlying issue of all individual sins, for believers or nonbelievers, is not believing or trusting in Jesus.

Our acts of sin are just the manifestations of the single inward heart condition of unbelief. Adam and Eve's eating of the forbidden fruit wasn't the real sin. It was the fact that they weren't trusting God anymore. They believed a talking snake more than their heavenly Father, who had only treated them well (Gen. 3:1–6).

The temptation Satan really offered Jesus wasn't to turn the stone into bread; it was to doubt what the heavenly Father had just said about Him (Matt. 3:17). That's why Satan said, "*If thou be the Son of God*" (Matt. 4:3 and 6). The Father said in an audible voice that Jesus was His Son (Matt. 3:17). Would Jesus trust the Father's word or do something to prove to Satan that He was the Son of God?

The sin that the Holy Spirit is reproving the world of is the sin of not believing on Jesus. All other acts of sin stem from this one problem. That's the sin that will send people to hell, not their individual acts. All the sins of the world have been paid for (1 John 2:2) except the sin of rejecting Jesus (John 3:18).

John 16:10

Of righteousness, because I go to my Father, and ye see me no more;

Most people read this in a way that really means the Holy Spirit reproves us of unrighteousness, but that is not what it says. The Holy Spirit convicts us that we are righteous through the new birth.

How many times have we seen people stand in church and say how the Holy Spirit has shown them how unrighteous they are? But people should be sharing how the Lord has convicted them that they are the righteousness of God in Christ (2 Cor. 5:21). That's normal Christianity. (Learn more about righteousness by reading Luke 18:10, Ephesians 4:24, and Romans 5:19 and 10:3.)

So, it's the ministry of the Holy Spirit to convict us that we are righteous through Jesus. Not many people receive that ministry because religious tradition and doctrines have made the Word of God (and this positive ministry of the Holy Spirit) of none effect (Mark 7:13).

There could be two ways of interpreting this. First, the Holy Spirit will now have to reveal to mankind what is righteous in the sight of God because Jesus is no longer visible to illustrate true righteousness to us. Second, this could mean that just as Jesus assured people that the goodness and mercy of God made them righteous by faith, not works, so now the Holy Spirit has taken over this ministry of bearing witness to their righteous relationship with the Father (1 John 5:13).

John 16:11

Of judgment, because the prince of this world is judged.

This is not saying that the Holy Spirit tells us we will be judged if we don't repent. It is speaking of the Holy Spirit showing us that Satan has been judged. The devil is the one who is judged, not us (John 12:32). We are the ones with the authority, not the devil. The Holy Spirit will remind us of that to encourage us. Praise the Lord!

This is not referring to the Holy Spirit revealing to people that they are going to hell if they don't repent. That would fall under the category of reproving the world of sin (John 16:9). Rather, this is speaking of the Holy Spirit assuring us that Satan has been judged and stripped of all authority over us. The Holy Spirit will assure us of our victory.

John 16:12

I have yet many things to say unto you, but ye cannot bear them now.

How often has the Lord had many things to say unto me, but I wasn't able to bear them? God, help me to have a sensitive heart so that I can receive everything You have for me.

Here, Jesus was saying that there were many things beyond this positive ministry of the Holy Spirit, which He had described in John 16:8–11 (see my notes at those verses), that He wanted to tell His disciples. But they weren't able to bear them at that time.

Today, the vast majority of Christians haven't understood these basic things that the Lord shared about the positive ministry of the Holy Spirit, so we certainly can't go on to greater things. This is a beginning point. If we don't receive this revelation, we can't receive other revelations.

As Jesus told His disciples this very night, the Holy Spirit would lead them into all truth (John 16:13). The disciples hadn't received the Holy Spirit yet, and therefore some of God's truths were hidden from them. Likewise, any believer who has not received the baptism of the Holy Spirit (see my notes at Acts 1:7–8 and 2:4) cannot receive the full revelation of what the Lord has for them.

The Lord doesn't reveal to us things that we cannot receive. This is why we sometimes fail to get a response from God when we are petitioning Him for answers. It's not that God is unwilling to respond; it's that we are unable to receive.

The way to overcome this hardness of heart (Mark 8:17) is to yield to the ministry of the Holy Spirit that Jesus began to describe in John 16:13.

John 16:13

> *Howbeit when he, the Spirit of truth, is come, he will guide you into all truth: for he shall not speak of himself; but whatsoever he shall hear,* that *shall he speak: and he will shew you things to come.*

What a wonderful promise! The Holy Spirit will show us things to come. If we will listen and receive this ministry of the Holy Spirit, this will change our lives. We can avoid many problems and take advantage of opportunities that we would otherwise miss. Jesus had just revealed a whole new way of relating to God in John 16:8–11.

The Holy Spirit wouldn't be convicting people of individual sins but of the singular sin of not believing on Jesus. That's the root of everything. And then the Holy Spirit would reveal to us that we are the righteousness of God in Christ (John 16:10) and that Satan has already been judged (John

16:11). Then Jesus said He wanted to tell them more, but they couldn't receive it yet (John 16:12).

Here, He spoke about how the Holy Spirit will lead them into all of these new things. So, receiving these revelations from the Lord that they were unable to receive at that time was dependent on them receiving this ministry of the Holy Spirit. If we don't receive this positive ministry of the Holy Spirit that Jesus revealed in John 16:8–11, our further revelation from the Holy Spirit will be blocked.

What a powerful truth! This elevates the necessity of understanding and receiving this positive ministry of the Holy Spirit to an essential ingredient of revelation knowledge.

A guide doesn't do everything for us but rather leads us. The Holy Spirit will lead us into all truth, but we have to follow. We have to go to the effort of studying, trusting that the Holy Spirit is leading us.

This was the fourth time Jesus emphasized the Holy Spirit as being the one to reveal the truths of God to the believer (see notes at John 14:26). In this instance, Jesus said the Holy Spirit would guide us into all truth. During this same night, Jesus said, "*Thy word is truth*" (John 17:17). Therefore, the Holy Spirit is specifically given to give revelation knowledge (Luke 2:26, John 6:45, and John 7:15) of God's Word.

Jesus had spoken of the ministry of the Holy Spirit many times before, but here He revealed that the Holy Spirit will show us things to come. Foreknowledge is one of the distinct characteristics of God alone (Is. 42:9, 45:11, and 46:9–10; Jer. 1:5; Matt. 6:8 and 24:36; Acts 15:18). Therefore, this is another witness to the Holy Spirit being part of the Godhead. Part of the Holy Spirit's ministry is to make this foreknowledge available to the believer. This does not automatically operate, but it can be appropriated by every Spirit-filled believer through faith. This is one of the most miraculous and beneficial ministries of the Holy Spirit, and also one of the least used.

John 16:14

He shall glorify me: for he shall receive of mine, and shall shew it *unto you.*

One of the keys to staying full of God is to glorify Him. To *glorify* means to value or esteem (Rom. 1:21).[15] So, the Holy Spirit will increase the value, or esteem, we place on Jesus. This cannot be done properly without the Holy Spirit, whose main job is to glorify Jesus.

The Greek word *anangello*, which was translated "*shew*" in this verse, means "to announce (in detail)."[16] So, the ministry of the Holy Spirit is to announce to us in detail what Jesus has done for us. Thank You, Holy Spirit! I receive that!

This was the second time in this discourse Jesus said that the Holy Spirit always testifies of or glorifies Jesus (John 15:26). This is one way to discern if someone or some doctrine is inspired by the Holy Spirit. John later drew on this truth as a test for discerning false prophets (1 John 4:2–3).

John 16:15

> *All things that the Father hath are mine: therefore said I, that he shall take of mine, and shall shew* it *unto you.*

Jesus was actually speaking in John 16:14 about the Holy Spirit revealing unto us the things of God, but He said He would "*receive of mine, and shall shew* it *unto you.*" In this verse, He revealed that receiving of Jesus and receiving of God are the same thing because everything that is true of the Father is true of the Son. This is a strong witness to the divinity of Jesus.

John 16:16

> *A little while, and ye shall not see me: and again, a little while, and ye shall see me, because I go to the Father.*

Jesus explained this in John 16:20–22. He was speaking of His death and resurrection. After His death, there would be a three-day period when they would not see Him. But that wouldn't be the end of the story. After three days, He would rise from the dead and appear to them on His way back to the Father.

John 16:17

> *Then said* some *of his disciples among themselves, What is this that he saith unto*

us, A little while, and ye shall not see me: and again, a little while, and ye shall see me: and, Because I go to the Father?

This same thing came up in the beginning of Jesus' discourse to His disciples this very night. He told them in John 14:4 that they knew where He was going and the way to get there. That occasioned Thomas saying that they didn't know where He was going, and if they didn't know where He was going, they certainly couldn't know the way (John 14:5).

Jesus rebuked them for not recognizing that He was the way, the truth, and the life (John 14:6). That may be the reason they were afraid to ask Jesus what He meant here (John 16:5).

We should go directly to the Lord with our questions and not inquire among ourselves about what He means.

John 16:18

They said therefore, What is this that he saith, A little while? we cannot tell what he saith.

It appears that the disciples were a little bit put out with Jesus' way of communicating with them, but they were afraid to say anything to Him. Jesus knew how they felt (John 16:19), and He admitted that He had been speaking to them in proverbs (John 16:25). He then promised that soon He would speak to them plainly of the Father (John 16:25).

Although we sometimes think that God's words are a little hard to understand (2 Peter 3:16), we should never make the mistake of inquiring among ourselves, like these disciples did (John 16:19), as to what the Lord means. We should go directly to Him and ask His wisdom, knowing that He will gladly give it without criticizing us (James 1:5).

John 16:19

Now Jesus knew that they were desirous to ask him, and said unto them, Do ye inquire among yourselves of that I said, A little while, and ye shall not see me: and again, a little while, and ye shall see me?

It's obvious from this passage that the disciples hadn't revealed their question to Jesus. They had been discussing this among themselves. But Jesus knew exactly what they were thinking (Ps. 139:1–6). The same thing is true with us. We need to take our questions directly to Him. It's the job of the Holy Spirit to announce to us in detail what Jesus has said and means (see my note at John 16:14).

John 16:20

Verily, verily, I say unto you, That ye shall weep and lament, but the world shall rejoice: and ye shall be sorrowful, but your sorrow shall be turned into joy.

It's always true that the things that cause the world to rejoice are odious to true believers. The believers' value systems are so different from the ungodly's that there is very little common ground. Yet those who truly trust in Jesus will get the last laugh. They will be comforted, while the ungodly are punished.

If Jesus' disciples had remembered this word, it would have given them hope during the three days when Jesus' body was in the grave. Their unbelief at the news of the resurrection indicates that they had forgotten this.

John 16:21

A woman when she is in travail hath sorrow, because her hour is come: but as soon as she is delivered of the child, she remembereth no more the anguish, for joy that a man is born into the world.

Jesus was using a physical example to illustrate the spiritual truth He was telling His disciples. Just as a woman experiences sorrow in delivering a baby but forgets it all in the great joy of bringing a child into the world, so Jesus' disciples would soon forget all their grief when they see Jesus resurrected from the dead.

John 16:22

And ye now therefore have sorrow: but I will see you again, and your heart shall rejoice, and your joy no man taketh from you.

No one can take our joy. We have to give it away.

Jesus spoke to His disciples so that their hearts would not be troubled (John 14:1) when they saw Him crucified, dead, and buried (John 16:1). Here, He told them that after their sorrow, they would see Him again and have great joy.

This is a very clear reference to His resurrection, and that would have encouraged them through that dark time if they would have received it. It appears that they were moved more by what they saw than by what Jesus said here.

John 16:23

> *And in that day ye shall ask me nothing. Verily, verily, I say unto you, Whatsoever ye shall ask the Father in my name, he will give* it *you.*

Ever since sin entered the world, man has always had to go through some mediator to approach God. This was because of God's holiness and man's sinfulness. In the Old Testament, sacrifices and priests were symbolic mediators. In the New Testament, Jesus is our High Priest mediator (Heb. 3:1 and 9:15).

However, Jesus' mediation was greater than anything that had ever existed before in that He not only was pure but also actually cleansed and purified the ones whom He was representing. Now we can come directly to the Father in His name. This is what Jesus was referring to, and it was a radical statement to the disciples.

It is awesome to think that we can commune directly with Almighty God, the creator of heaven and earth, but that is exactly what Jesus provided for. In John 16:26–27, Jesus revealed that He had reconciled man to God so completely that the disciples wouldn't have to pray to Him and then have Him relay the message to the Father, but they could go directly to the Father Himself.

John 16:24

Hitherto have ye asked nothing in my name: ask, and ye shall receive, that your joy may be full.

Prior to the death and resurrection of our Lord Jesus, Old Testament saints didn't have a Savior. They, in a sense, were asking in their own names. They appealed to the mercy of

God, as demonstrated in the sacrifices that covered their sins, but there was no real atonement.

When Jesus died, He made the real atonement that all of the Old Testament sacrifices illustrated. He became our Savior, and now we can do much more than approach God in our names, based on our performances. We can ask and receive from the Lord in Jesus' name, based on His performance. Praise the Lord!

This is the difference between approaching the Lord in the flesh and approaching Him in the Spirit. Using the name of Jesus means that we are claiming the righteousness of Jesus as what makes us worthy to receive. It means that we are depending on the grace of God and not our performances.

Those who ask but believe it is dependent on how well they perform are actually taking the name of the Lord in vain. It doesn't matter if they end every prayer with "in Jesus' name." If they aren't standing in the grace of God, they aren't using the name of Jesus correctly.

The proper way to pray is to the Father in the name of Jesus. While Jesus was on the earth, the disciples asked Him for whatever they needed, and Jesus would ask the Father and get it for them. Here, He was saying that they should not ask Him anymore, but they should take their requests directly to the Father.

Asking in the name of Jesus means that God treats our requests the same as He would if Jesus was personally making the petition. Therefore, we can expect the same treatment from God as Jesus would get. In the business world, that is called the power of attorney.

Those who pray in the name of Jesus but then doubt that God would answer their prayers because they aren't holy enough are taking the name of Jesus in vain. If people pray in Jesus' name, then it is His holiness that God looks at and not theirs.

John 16:25

These things have I spoken unto you in proverbs: but the time cometh, when I shall no more speak unto you in proverbs, but I shall shew you plainly of the Father.

Matthew 13:10–15 reveals why Jesus spoke in parables. In John 10:6, the same Greek word, *paroimia*, that was translated "*proverbs*" here, was translated "*parable*."[17] So it appears that parables and proverbs are at least related if not the same.

John 16:26

> *At that day ye shall ask in my name: and I say not unto you, that I will pray the Father for you:*

We don't have to pray to Jesus and then ask Him to relay our requests on to His Father and put in a good word for us. No! Jesus so totally cleansed us that we can now go directly to the Father through what He did for us. That's what it means when we pray in Jesus' name. This is a privilege that none of us deserve on our own merits but that every true believer in Jesus has received as a grace gift.

John 16:27

> *For the Father himself loveth you, because ye have loved me, and have believed that I came out from God.*

Many people see God as a harsh God whom Jesus has to constantly appease to keep peace in the family. But here, Jesus revealed God the Father as loving us (1 John 4:8 and 16) just because we love Jesus. Those who are in love with His Son have God the Father in love with them.

John 16:28

I came forth from the Father, and am come into the world: again, I leave the world, and go to the Father.

Jesus didn't just begin His life when He was born in a stable to Mary. He preexisted with the Father before the world began (John 17:5 and Col. 1:16–17). This is a clear testimony to the deity of Christ. Jesus existed with God the Father before He came to earth. Here, He said that He was going back to the Father.

John 16:29

His disciples said unto him, Lo, now speakest thou plainly, and speakest no proverb.

The disciples finally understood that Jesus was speaking of leaving this world and going back to the Father. But they didn't understand that this would take place through Jesus dying, being buried, and being raised on the third day. So, they were still clueless as Jesus revealed in His next statements.

These disciples would have done well to follow the admonition of Proverbs 17:28. It seems like the only time they opened their mouths was to change feet. They may have understood a little better what Jesus was trying to tell them, but Jesus' continued discourse with them reveals that they still didn't have a clue.

John 16:30

> *Now are we sure that thou knowest all things, and needest not that any man should ask thee: by this we believe that thou camest forth from God.*

This is amazing! Jesus had performed miracles like no one who had ever walked on the earth before. He had spoken like no one had ever spoken before. Yet those things hadn't convinced the disciples that He was from God. Here, they were saying that they were finally convinced, but Jesus' further discourse with them showed that they were still in unbelief.

John 16:31

Jesus answered them, Do ye now believe?

These disciples were still struggling with unbelief. Jesus' prophecy in John 16:32 and their actions when they all forsook Him and fled (Matt. 26:56 and Mark 14:50) proved that.

John 16:32

> *Behold, the hour cometh, yea, is now come, that ye shall be scattered, every man to his own, and shall leave me alone: and yet I am not alone, because the Father is with me.*

Every one of these disciples forsook Jesus (Matt. 26:56 and Mark 14:50). Jesus' statements here reveal that He knew this would happen, yet He loved them and served them. Jesus is faithful to us even when we aren't faithful to Him (2 Tim. 2:13).

Jesus was so one with His Father that even when everyone else forsook Him, He was not alone. Likewise, we need to draw so close to the Lord that His presence overwhelms any rejection that might come from people.

John 16:33

> *These things I have spoken unto you, that in me ye might have peace. In the world ye shall have tribulation: but be of good cheer; I have overcome the world.*

The Lord clearly stated that we will have trouble in this world, but we can still be of good cheer because He has overcome the world. There is no justification for us being defeated. God's provision is greater than all our needs. Notice that our peace is dependent upon the words He has spoken unto us. It's through God's Word that we renew our minds (Rom. 12:2). The Lord keeps us in perfect peace when our minds are stayed upon Him through taking heed to His Word (Is. 26:3).

In John 16:1, Jesus said He was speaking these things so that the disciples would not be offended. By comparing this statement with that first verse, it can be said that losing our peace is being offended. If we can keep our peace, we can keep from being offended. "*Thou wilt keep* him *in perfect peace,* whose *mind* is *stayed* on thee: *because he trusteth in thee*" (Is. 26:3).

Jesus said we would have tribulation. He did not say that He was the one bringing the tribulation or what the tribulation would be, but He said it would come. Then He made the amazing statement that in the midst of tribulation, we were to be of good cheer.

The world has joy and happiness directly proportional to circumstances. Bad circumstances produce depression and sorrow, while good circumstances produce joy and peace. That's bondage, and that does not have to be the case with us as Christians. Our joy is not dependent on things but rather on the person of Jesus Christ. He is our peace (Eph. 2:14) and joy.

The way we take advantage of this joy and peace in the midst of tribulation is to have our minds and hearts stayed on things above and not on things of this earth (Col. 3:1–2). The invisible things of God are eternal, while all the visible problems that we see are only temporary (2 Cor. 4:17–18). All the problems of this life grow very dim when compared to the glory of God that has become ours through Jesus.

Receive Jesus as Your Savior

Choosing to receive Jesus Christ as your Lord and Savior is the most important decision you'll ever make!

God's Word promises, "*That if thou shalt confess with thy mouth the Lord Jesus, and shalt believe in thine heart that God hath raised him from the dead, thou shalt be saved. For with the heart man believeth unto righteousness; and with the mouth confession is made unto salvation*" (Rom. 10:9–10). "*For whosoever shall call upon the name of the Lord shall be saved*" (Rom. 10:13). By His grace, God has already done everything to provide salvation. Your part is simply to believe and receive.

Pray out loud: "Jesus, I acknowledge that I've sinned and need to receive what you did for the forgiveness of my sins. I confess that You are my Lord and Savior. I believe in my heart that God raised You from the dead. By faith in Your Word, I receive salvation now. Thank You for saving me."

The very moment you commit your life to Jesus Christ, the truth of His Word instantly comes to pass in your spirit. Now that you're born again, there's a brand-new you!

Please contact us and let us know that you've prayed to receive Jesus as your Savior. We'd like to send you some free materials to help you on your new journey. Call our Helpline: **719-635-1111** (available 24 hours a day, seven days a week) to speak to a staff member who is here to help you understand and grow in your new relationship with the Lord.

Welcome to your new life!

Receive the Holy Spirit

As His child, your loving heavenly Father wants to give you the supernatural power you need to live a new life. "*For every one that asketh receiveth; and he that seeketh findeth; and to him that knocketh it shall be opened...how much more shall your heavenly Father give the Holy Spirit to them that ask him?*" (Luke 11:10–13).

All you have to do is ask, believe, and receive!

Pray this: "Father, I recognize my need for Your power to live a new life. Please fill me with Your Holy Spirit. By faith, I receive it right now. Thank You for baptizing me. Holy Spirit, You are welcome in my life."

Some syllables from a language you don't recognize will rise up from your heart to your mouth (1 Cor. 14:14). As you speak them out loud by faith, you're releasing God's power from within and building yourself up in the spirit (1 Cor. 14:4). You can do this whenever and wherever you like.

It doesn't really matter whether you felt anything or not when you prayed to receive the Lord and His Spirit. If you believed in your heart that you received, then God's Word promises you did. "*Therefore I say unto you, What things soever ye desire, when ye pray, believe that ye receive* them, *and ye shall have* them" (Mark 11:24). God always honors His Word—believe it!

We would like to rejoice with you, pray with you, and answer any questions to help you understand more fully what has taken place in your life!

Please contact us to let us know that you've prayed to be filled with the Holy Spirit and to request the book *The New You & the Holy Spirit*. This book will explain in more detail about the benefits of being filled with the Holy Spirit and speaking in tongues. Call our Helpline: **719-635-1111** (available 24 hours a day, seven days a week).

Call for Prayer

If you need prayer for any reason, you can call our Helpline, 24 hours a day, seven days a week at **719-635-1111**. A trained prayer minister will answer your call and pray with you.

Every day, we receive testimonies of healings and other miracles from our Helpline, and we are ministering God's nearly-too-good-to-be-true message of the Gospel to more people than ever. So, I encourage you to call today!

About the Author

Andrew Wommack's life was forever changed the moment he encountered the supernatural love of God on March 23, 1968. As a renowned Bible teacher and author, Andrew has made it his mission to change the way the world sees God.

Andrew's vision is to go as far and deep with the Gospel as possible. His message goes far through the Gospel Truth television program, which is available to over half the world's population. The message goes deep through discipleship at Charis Bible College, headquartered in Woodland Park, Colorado. Founded in 1994, Charis has campuses across the United States and around the globe.

Andrew also has an extensive library of teaching materials in print, audio, and video. More than 200,000 hours of free teachings can be accessed at **awmi.net**.

Endnotes

1. *Strong's Definitions*, s.v. "οἰκία" ("oikia"), accessed April 8, 2024, https://www.blueletterbible.org/lexicon/g3614/kjv/tr/0-1/

2. *Vine's Expository Dictionary of New Testament Words*, s.v. "allos/heteros," accessed April 9, 2024, https://www.blueletterbible.org/lexicon/g243/kjv/tr/0-1/

3. *Strong's Definitions*, s.v. "ὀρφανός" ("orphanos"), accessed April 9, 2024, https://www.blueletterbible.org/lexicon/g3737/kjv/tr/0-1/

4. *Blue Letter Bible*, s.v. "θεωρέω" ("theōreō"), accessed April 9, 2024, https://www.blueletterbible.org/lexicon/g2334/kjv/tr/0-1/

5. *Strong's Definitions*, s.v. "εἴδω" ("eidō"), accessed April 9, 2024, https://www.blueletterbible.org/lexicon/g1492/kjv/tr/0-1/ and Strong's Definitions, s.v. "ὀπτάνομαι" ("optanomai"), accessed April 9, 2024, https://www.blueletterbible.org/lexicon/g3700/kjv/tr/0-1/

6. *American Heritage Dictionary of the English Language*, s.v. "manifest," accessed April 9, 2024, https://ahdictionary.com/word/search.html?q=manifest

7. *Strong's Definitions*, s.v. "ἐμφανίζω" ("emphanizō"), accessed April 9, 2024, https://www.blueletterbible.org/lexicon/g1718/kjv/tr/0-1/

8. *Strong's Definitions*, s.v. "δειλιάω" ("deiliaō"), accessed April 9, 2024, https://www.blueletterbible.org/lexicon/g1168/kjv/tr/0-1/

9. *Strong's Definitions*, s.v. "καθαίρω" ("kathairō"), accessed April 9, 2024, https://www.blueletterbible.org/lexicon/g2508/kjv/tr/0-1/

10. *Strong's Definitions*, s.v. "καθαρός" ("katharos"), accessed April 9, 2024, https://www.blueletterbible.org/lexicon/g2513/kjv/tr/0-1/

11. *Strong's Definitions*, s.v. "καθαίρω" ("kathairō"), accessed April 9, 2024, https://www.blueletterbible.org/lexicon/g2508/kjv/tr/0-1/

12. *Strong's Definitions*, s.v. "μένω" ("menō"), accessed April 9, 2024, https://www.blueletterbible.org/lexicon/g3306/kjv/tr/0-1/

13. *American Heritage Dictionary of the English Language*, s.v. "abide," accessed April 25, 2024, https://ahdictionary.com/word/search.html?q=abide

14. *Vine's Expository Dictionary of New Testament Words*, s.v. "sumphero," accessed April 10, 2024, https://www.blueletterbible.org/lexicon/g4851/kjv/tr/0-1/

15. *Blue Letter Bible*, s.v. "δοξάζω" ("doxazō"), accessed April 10, 2024, https://www.blueletterbible.org/lexicon/g1392/kjv/tr/0-1/

16. *Strong's Definitions*, s.v. "ἀναγγέλλω" ("anangellō"), accessed April 10, 2024, https://www.blueletterbible.org/lexicon/g312/kjv/tr/0-1/

17. *Blue Letter Bible*, s.v. "παροιμία" ("paroimia"), accessed April 10, 2024, https://www.blueletterbible.org/lexicon/g3942/kjv/tr/0-1/

Contact Information

Andrew Wommack Ministries, Inc.

PO Box 3333
Colorado Springs, CO 80934-3333
info@awmi.net
awmi.net

Helpline: 719-635-1111 (available 24/7)

Charis Bible College

info@charisbiblecollege.org
844-360-9577
CharisBibleCollege.org

For a complete list of all of our offices, visit **awmi.net/contact-us**.

Connect with us on social media.

God Wants You Well book

In this book, Andrew reveals the truth of what God's unconditional love and grace has already provided. Healing is a big part of that provision. Unfortunately, religion tells you that God uses sickness to teach you something, even suggesting that it's a blessing. That's just not true. God wants you well! If you or someone you know needs healing, this book is for you.

The Believer's Authority book

Dig into the Word with Andrew as he uncovers the spiritual significance of your choices, words, and actions. Explore how they affect your ability to resist Satan's attacks and receive God's best. Discover the powerful truths behind true spiritual authority and begin seeing real results.

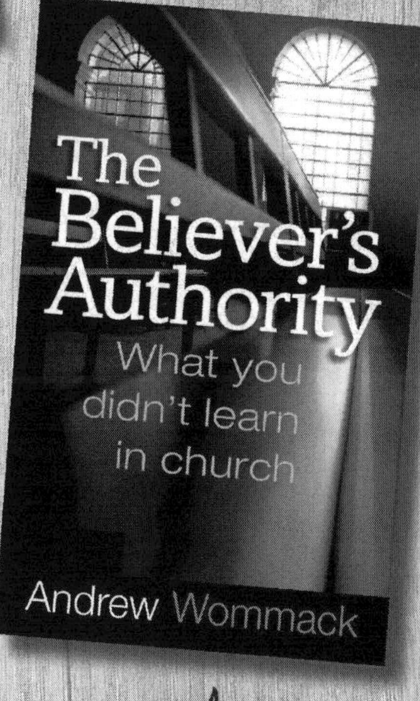

Discover these products and more by scanning the QR code or visiting **store.awmi.net**.

ANDREW WOMMACK MINISTRIES